Harry Turner has been a salesman most of his working life. His first job, as a canned food salesman in London's East End, was followed by a five year stint in Fleet Street, selling advertising space for several national newspapers. In 1962, after two years as Advertising Manager on *TV International Magazine*, he joined Westward Television Sales Department where he spent 19 years, becoming Sales Director in 1972. In 1981, he became Director of Sales and Marketing for Television South West, and in 1985 was appointed Managing Director. He is also a Vice-Chairman of The Advertising Association, a member of The Advertising Advisory Committee in the Government's Central Office of Information, and a Fellow of The Royal Society of Arts.

A prolific writer, Harry Turner's stories have been adapted for both television and radio. He also contributes regularly to 'Campaign', 'Marketing Week' and 'Broadcast'.

So You Want To Be A Sales Manager?

Harry Turner

ARROW BOOKS
AN ARROW ORIGINAL

Arrow Books Limited
62–65 Chandos Place, London WC2N 4NW

An imprint of Century Hutchinson Limited

London Melbourne Sydney Auckland
Johannesburg and agencies throughout
the world

First published in Arrow Books 1988

© Harry Turner 1988

This book is sold subject to the condition that it shall
not, by way of trade or otherwise, be lent, resold, hired
out, or otherwise circulated without the publisher's prior
consent in any form of binding or cover other than that in
which it is published and without a similar condition
including this condition being imposed on the subsequent
purchaser

Typeset by Input Typesetting Ltd, London

Printed and bound in Great Britain by
Anchor Brendon Limited, Tiptree, Essex

ISBN 0 09 956440 8

Contents

Introduction

My thirty years as a salesman have been crammed with incident. A lot more actually happens to successful salespeople than it does to fire-eaters, trick cyclists or nose surgeons. This may sound like an exaggeration, but ask yourself honestly, how many fire-eaters can you name in *your* neighbourhood who lead interesting lives? The trouble with the sort of specialists I've listed is, of course, the narrowness of their experience. Nose surgeons are not necessarily bad people, but when you've gazed up one set of flared nostrils with a little pencil torch it's pretty well downhill from then on. Likewise trick cyclists.

Salespeople, however, span a wide range of human endeavour. They are in there, pitching to heads of state to win monumental contracts for giant irrigation systems; they are poised in the elegant lobbies of great hotels waiting to clinch deals over a whole cornucopia of products and services – rare books, uncut diamonds, oil wells, medical supplies, motor cars and airport constructions.

They are also foot-slogging in the huge council estates in Glasgow and Nottingham and North London, selling insurance and double glazing and children's toys and cheap cosmetics.

At every minute in every hour, somewhere in the world, countless acts of salesmanship are being consummated by men and women as various as the goods and services they are offering.

During my thirty years, I have pounded the pavements of London's dockland, exhilarated with a single 'Yes' from a semi-literate café proprietor who usually treated sales-people like lepers, and I have shaken hands on a single three-hundred-thousand-pound order over smoked salmon in the Ritz. I've also done a hell of a lot of business in between those two extremes.

If you are a salesman or saleswoman already and you aspire to higher things, then this book will provide signposts that will guide you on that perilous journey, show you how to bolster your self-confidence and guide you in acquiring those work skills that exhilarate, making life flash by like a runaway train.

1
So you want to be a sales manager?

One of the toughest steps on the career salesperson's ladder is that which leads upwards to a sales *management* post.

Not all great salespeople make good managers. Indeed, there is much evidence to suggest that their failure rate is somewhat higher than in other branches of industry. Why is this so?

Well, to begin with, the qualities required in a manager are markedly different to those of a high-flying, individualistic salesperson. Pure selling is a one-to-one, occasionally lonely business, and the successful practitioner learns primarily self-motivation and to carry the customer along on a tide of eloquent persuasion.

Management is far less cut and dried. The newly promoted salesperson will have to learn a whole raft of fresh disciplines and priorities that in some cases *go completely against the grain* of what has been learnt hitherto.

Let's examine a few examples.

A pure salesperson, by the very nature of the calling, has no need to understand such things as group motivation, cost control, staff training, the construction of incentive schemes and the establishment of sales conference programmes. He or she zeroes in on the product or service *and* the anticipated reaction of the clients. The salesperson develops an individual style that suits his or her clearly defined responsibilities and learns to accept that such things as 'target-setting' and the 'construction of commission scales' are areas dealt with by 'them' – i.e. sales management.

In the next few chapters we're going to examine in detail how a salesman or saleswoman can prepare themselves for positions in management. Before reading on, be scrupulously honest with yourself.

Do you sincerely want to trade-in the relative freedom of being an *individual* salesperson for the tightly disciplined role of sales manager? You do. Excellent. You're not sure? Too warm and comfortable on your familiar patch? Well, read on anyway; you might better understand some of the stratagems employed by those cunning bosses back at head office.

The first thing to realise is that you are now responsible for the *sales effectiveness* of other people. Your own personal skills as an ex-salesperson are less important than your ability to create an environment in which others will excel. For many new managers this is a bitter pill to swallow. Their instincts tell them that if only they could find the time they could out-pitch all of their sales team and show them how it should *really* be done. Their reasoning is simple: I have been promised my new position because of my brilliance as an order-getter. Therefore I must continue to outshine my staff in one-to-one sales situations. Understandable, I hear you say! Indeed, but it is also absolutely fatal.

I have worked for sales managers who actually hated managing but loved selling. They could never keep their hands off the detail and constantly usurped the daily tasks of the people in their employ. The net result of all this ego-tripping, for such it is, was a gradual demoralisation of the sales force. How would you like it if your boss kept leaping into your shoes and trumpeting, 'Now that's how it ought to be done'? You'd hate it. You'd develop a neurotic twitch and you would experience a draining of confidence and self-esteem. You might even start dreaming about boiling your sales manager's head in a bucket of oil. And who could blame you? How then do newly promoted sales managers wean themselves away from the coal-face and start behaving like executives? Initially you must take stock of your *own* qualities. You must ask yourself the following questions – and answer them honestly.

'Am I a broad-canvas merchant? Do I excel at looking at the big picture, and am I possessed of just a touch of forward vision?'

or

'Am I a wizard at detail, never happier or more effective than when poring over the small print of individual sales figures?'

or

'Am I a "people" manager, constantly "visible" to the troops, giving off body-warmth and exuding palpable enthusiasm?'

or

'Do I prefer the safety of my new office, snugly comfortable behind my big new desk, my most treasured confidante being either my secretary or the telephone?'

Managers do fall broadly into categories – and it is vital to recognise what sort of manager you are likely to be. If you are obsessed by detail, neatness and administration, your style is unlikely to set your sales team's adrenaline foaming through their veins. Salespeople are like actors, remember; they need a constant mixture of praise and pressure – and they need *positive* leadership. For the esoteric, faintly bureaucratic manager, therefore, a deputy manager who is a gregarious contrast is essential. *Somebody* has to press the flesh, slap the backs, swap the jokes, apply the boot to the recalcitrant backside and generally hustle

11

the troops. Without direct involvement, your sales team will wither from lack of sustenance – believe me.

But direct involvement isn't the same thing as pettifogging interference, and the sooner you recognise the subtle difference the better an executive you will become.

Let's assume that you are *not* a desk-wallah and you prefer to study and perfect the art of inspirational leadership – or, as I prefer to describe it, *up-front management*. Once again, you must ensure that you have either a detail-conscious deputy, or a skilled and well-disciplined secretary. Don't knock administration and book-keeping – *somebody's* got to do it.

Thus, confident in your 'secretariat' who will mind the shop while you strut your stuff, you must then roll up your sleeves and set about your chosen task with unflagging gusto. And your chosen task is to create – by sheer force of personal will – an environment in which *each* and *every* salesperson under your direction can grow to their full potential. How precisely do you achieve this? Sounds pretty glib after all, doesn't it?

Well, your primary goal is to raise the morale of the sales team – oh yes, there's *always* room for improvement here. They must believe that the company values them, that the company is goal-orientated and appreciative of their efforts. They must believe that exceptional rewards will follow exceptional results. You'll bust liver, lights and bloodvessels to see they are properly remunerated, won't you? You will be the centre point of raising the company's profile in the market-place. You will make yourself known personally to ALL the senior people in client companies with whom you do business. This is so important as to be worth repeating.

You will make yourself known personally to ALL the senior people in client companies with whom you do business.

12

When your reps hit a stonewall – and *every* rep does sooner or later – they look to *you* to find a way round it.

This is the moment when your scrupulously constructed list of personal contacts comes in handy. You can phone a senior man or woman in the company concerned and try the diplomatic approach. If sales managers can't massage their way out of an impasse, then who the hell can? Be most careful not to usurp your rep's own contacts – this will sap his or her confidence and raise the expectations of the buyer, who will side-step the rep and deal directly with you in future.

This will be counter-productive, and before you know it, you'll be on the receiving end of countless calls from junior clients who look upon their right to go 'right to the top' as inalienable.

It will also prove to be a pain in the arse for you *and* your salespeople. So make your own special contacts. Go as high as you feel comfortable with – chairmen, even. Play golf with your contacts. Flatter their wives, admire their backhand at tennis, keep them warm, make them feel good about your company and *never call in a favour* unless your back is against the wall and all other avenues have been explored and found to be irrevocably blocked.

Meantime, your sales team will expect you to exude confidence and enthusiasm *at all times* – even when you've been out till four a.m. with the managing director of that huge client in the suburbs of Birmingham and your eyes feel like two hard-boiled eggs dipped in grit.

You will *never* drift into the office looking like death. You will always glow with energy and have a smile for that junior salesperson who is feeling nervous and in need of a boost.

Walk among the team on the sales floor. Show yourself. Talk. Ask. Let them *know* your juices are rising and that they can draw energy and strength from your abundant supply. Never underestimate the electrifying power of old-fashioned leadership. If you genuinely *like* salespeople – as I do – it will be easy to identify with their fears and hopes, and you'll find that you can transmit invisible waves of energy and determination which will set them about their tasks with renewed vigour.

Always ask yourself, 'What *more* can I do to make a contribution towards that ideal environment where each salesperson is hyped-up and super-charged with the will to win?'

It's no easy job, maintaining that kind of heady, let's-conquer-the-world atmosphere, and in reality there will be days when the sales floor will be about as frothy as a lead balloon.

It's your role to lift spirits again – by *listening* to their grumbles and worries. And it's your role to be the problem-solver. It's one hell of a job, whichever way you slice it. You'll need the constitution and resilience of an ox. And every Friday when you go home you will ask yourself four questions:

Have I worked to the *maximum* of my ability?

Have I succeeded in *most* of my tasks?

Have I had *fun?*

Am I absolutely exhausted?

If you're going to make it to the very top in management, then your answer will be a big Yes to all four.

You still want to be a sales manager? Good.

The next few chapters will dissect such vital subjects as criticism, praise, goal-setting, hiring and firing people, and much, much more.

2
How to hire a good salesperson

Hiring people can be hell. If they don't work out, it's *your* reputation as much as anybody else's that will be on the chopping block. So treat the job interview with great care and as much preparation as time will permit. *Read* the application and hunt for clues. Is the aspiring sales wizard all bull and no brain – and how can you tell before you've even met?

In my experience certain clues do exist. For example does the letter of application ramble on about irrelevant topics?

I mean, does his or her interest in tropical goldfish and the films of Jean-Luc Godard have the smallest bearing on the selling of rivets or baked beans (or whatever it is you are selling)? Does he or she write legibly? Trivial, perhaps, but a strong pointer to the kind of man or woman you're about to meet. Good salespeople have a strong desire to be *understood*, even in writing. So look for directness and simplicity in style, neatness of execution or, better still, a crisply typed letter with no spelling mistakes.

Beware the overkill. By that I mean the applicant who is interested in becoming your rep in Bootle but lists as hobbies: roller-skating, Buddhism, botany, shark-fishing, weight-lifting, ancient Persian and the restoration of Norman church towers.

This sort of phoney paragon will probably write an accompanying letter that contains faintly impertinent statements like: 'I look forward to hearing from you at the soonest opportunity as my father is a director of one of your largest clients.'

I've had a few letters like that in my time and they are a dead give-away. The writer always turns out to be a chinless wimp or a bombastic head-butter. You can do without either.

Do not be overawed by academic qualifications unless they are relevant to your own business. A degree in engineering is fine if you are engaged in the marketing of technical equipment. Honours in economics can be splendid if your business is selling financial products like insurance-linked investments. A degree in medieval Russian, painstakingly studied over four years, could actually be counter-productive if you expect this flower of academic brilliance to blossom among the potential purchasers of double glazing in Slough.

What a university degree means to most reasonable sales managers is that the applicant has displayed a fair amount of intellectual discipline. He or she will therefore be a fast learner and probably quite articulate. These are very positive qualities and every good salesperson should possess them.

The letter of application itself may be an original, written with passion and conviction, but beware the looming ego – watch out for too many 'I *wants*' in the text. Does the writer even hint at what benefits you, the employer, may expect if you hire them?

If no such hint exists, be very careful. Good salespeople, remember, sell 'benefits' and 'positive rewards' to their customers, and a job application is, after all, just another sales pitch.

When you have read the application, ask yourself this question: Would I pay a fiver out of my own pocket to actually *meet* this person? It's not a bad test. Most applications, it is true, will chalk up a negative but a few, just a very few, will so arouse your curiosity that you *would* be happy to peel off a banknote just to satisfy it.

The interview itself, assuming the young hopeful actually gets that far, is the real testing ground. Job interviews are, I'm afraid, artificial set pieces with two strangers on best behaviour straining every sinew to make a good impression. Oh yes, the interviewer too. If you've ever interviewed anybody you'll know what I mean.

First impressions *are* important. In selling they can make the difference between an order or a rejection, so here are a few things to look for.

1 Physical appearance: Is the applicant neat, or untidy? Overdressed or shabby? If he or she looks like a hippy *or* a millionaire estate agent, beware!
2 Cleanliness: Look for dirty fingernails or unpolished shoes. And dodgy teeth. Salesmen use their mouths a lot.
3 Is the handshake firm or is it like grasping a dead halibut?
4 Is the handshake vice-like, causing your knuckles to crack?
5 Are you getting a *genuine* smile on first meeting? Or a pained grimace? Or even a scowl?
6 How does the applicant sit? Easily and comfortably, one leg neatly crossed over the other, is ideal.
7 Or perched on the edge of the chair displaying four inches of either white calf (male) or an elaborate suspender belt (female). (Not good. Fun maybe, but definitely not good.)
8 Voice. Is the first sentence uttered pleasing to the ear or does it sound like a buzz-saw cleaving its way through sheet-metal?
9 Does the applicant let *you* start the talking? If not,

this is a bad sign. He or she is *your* guest, remember. And salespeople should always be prepared to let the host or client kick off any formal meeting.

10 Gestures. A good salesman or saleswoman will use their hands while talking. It's a natural consequence of a strong personality – but watch out for wild gesticulations and fist clenching. You could be on the verge of hiring a neurotic.

11 Vocabulary. Give the man or woman time to *develop* their replies to your questions. By listening patiently you will see how their conversation flows and whether or not they have a good command of English. Do not be impressed by buzz-words or trendy phrases like: 'I know I could provide a meaningful interface with your customers at this moment in time because I am a sincere, committed-type person with fire in my belly and a mission to explain.'

12 Show the door *at once* to any person who knocks the company he works for – or his employer personally. You want *positive* vibes, not negative ones. Above all else, try and let the applicant show their personality. Let him or her talk about their favourite hobby – this will give you a clue as to their *'enthusiasm potential'*. A man or woman who cannot enthuse about their pet subject can *never* become an effective salesperson.

Another worthwhile quality you should be looking for is inquisitiveness. Not the silly sort like 'Excuse me, Mr Turner, where did you buy those fancy cuff-links?' Or 'How can I get a dinner date with your secretary?' But serious questions about the job, the company, the market and the future.

Any applicant worth his or her salt should have done a fair amount of homework about you and your organisation. Don't be afraid to press for specific answers. He or she should have at least a passing knowledge of your product or service card, and should be prepared to give an opinion on your current press or television advertising campaign.

Prospective salespeople should have made it their business to understand what you can actually offer to your customers, and they should be prepared – even eager – to list its virtues or its USP (Unique Selling Proposition).

Don't expect detailed product knowledge – that would be unfair – but the ability to absorb information quickly is a trait you should be looking for in salespeople. Dumb, blank-faced applicants who coyly excuse their total ignorance by whimpering 'I haven't had time to read up on your company, but I'm willing to learn' are not good news. Passive people you need like a hole in the head. What you seek are self-starters, go-getters, *enthusiasts*.

Finally, and I am afraid unscientifically, you will have to ask yourself, Is the chemistry right with this person? Can *I* work with him or her? Perhaps more important, can they work harmoniously with the rest of the sales team – one bad apple, remember!

If your finely honed instincts sound the all-clear, and you are satisfied with the more formal parts of the interview, don't relax – the only real proof that you have made the right choice is *after* you have hired that person, and maybe as long as six months after you've hired them. So as you shake hands and make a mental note to inform the personnel department that you've recruited the best thing since digital watches or self-raising doughnuts, you'd better contrive to keep at least two fingers crossed – just in case.

3
Firing people – an occasional but necessary evil

There will come a time in every sales manager's life when he or she is faced with the prospect of firing somebody. This is never a pleasant experience. Any manager who claims to be unmoved by the act of separating another person from their job is either a liar or an insensitive brute.

In my early career, before employment protection legislation came into force, men and women could be, and too frequently *were*, unceremoniously dumped at the whim of an autocratic executive.

As an employer myself, I welcome the more civilised approach to this age-old problem. When you ask someone to leave, you are not merely taking away their job, you are cutting deep into their self-esteem and this can, if handled maladroitly, do more long-term damage than any financial deprivation.

So, before you exercise your ultimate executive power, ask yourself how *you* would like to be treated if, God forbid, the boot was on the other foot. Let us examine the only valid reasons why you should have to fire somebody.

1 Misconduct. (Theft, violence, cheating etc)
2 *Continuous* failure to perform prescribed duties or tasks set by the management. In the case of sales personnel this usually means a permanent decline in sales figures, particularly if the trend throughout the rest of the team is upwards. Be most scrupulous, however, that

20

the duff performance is not the result of bad accounts or an uneven distribution of territory. A rep allocated Macclesfield as an area in which to sell catamarans is hardly likely to set your sales figures rocketing off the wall chart.

3 A serious contraction of your business which necessitates selective redundancies. Beware, though; making an employee redundant is *not* the same as firing him.

Never dismiss an employee during an argument or when either of you is in a state of agitation. Emotion should play no part in the scenario. However angry you may feel as a result of provocation, idleness, carelessness or whatever, you *must be coolly dispassionate* when the final denouement takes place.

You will, of course, have observed the procedure of statutory *written* warnings *before* the last resort – won't you? Although formal dismissal *must* be in writing, it is a cowardly manager who delivers the coup de grâce by means of a buff envelope left on the employee's desk.

You must be prepared to look the unfortunate straight in the eye and explain, carefully and quietly, why he or she must leave the company. Be sure to have them sitting down when you break the news. (Although the majority of staff who are about to be fired *know* what's coming.) It is discourteous and archaic to squat behind your desk while the wretched victim stands uneasily before you like a prisoner in the dock.

Occasionally, if your legal advisers suggest it, you may require a third party as witness in the room during your terminal conversation. Try not to make the meeting more personal than you have to. And be firm, as well as gentle.

Your objective is to remove the person from your company, not destroy them. Do not allow an argument to develop, however low-key. Once the decision has been made to fire an employee, it is *non-negotiable*.

Managers who backtrack as a result of emotional blackmail (tears, sobs, rending of garments, offers of sexual favours – not unknown, so don't laugh – even bribes of cash) will lose all credibility with their staff and their management colleagues.

Try and make the severance terms as generous as the company will allow. A recently fired salesperson who is pinched for money will bad-mouth you and your organisation and do your reputation no good whatsoever.

Be firm in avoiding farewell parties *on the premises* for people who have been dismissed. Indeed, you should steel yourself for a 'clean kill' and ask the employee to clear their desk and leave within a half-day *at the very most*. You must avoid the walking-wounded syndrome where a newly ex-staff member metaphorically bleeds all over his colleagues, drumming up sympathy, resentment and unease. I cannot emphasise too strongly how critical this is. In a sales team, morale is a fragile commodity and nothing wrong-foots a good salesperson more quickly than the badly managed dismissal of a colleague. Quite often, in sales organisations, you will get advance warning signals of a rep who is beginning to under-perform. Not *necessarily* from scrutinising the monthly sales figures, either. A chain is as strong as its weakest link and good salespeople can sniff out the 'passenger' or problem rep in their midst with the tenacity of trained bloodhounds.

As always, prevention is better than cure, and if a previously satisfactory salesman or saleswoman suddenly starts to produce wobbly results there may be a deeper, less obvious reason than mere lack of effort. It could be a personal problem – money worries, conflict with other sales colleagues, or even an obstinately difficult client. It's the manager's job to dig deep and find out what has caused the decline in performance and, initially at least, restore the employee's confidence. It's never too early to have that one-to-one chat if you suspect that one of your sales-people is about to go into a downward swerve.

It is *not* a good policy to use the threat of dismissal as a negotiating weapon, unless it is a formal, considered warning – *in writing* – and you are absolutely certain that you are so close to the end that you have no real alternative.

There are a few simple ground rules about how to conduct yourself as a manager when you are required to terminate a sales representative's employment. Here's a checklist I have used myself. First of all the *don'ts*.

1 *Don't* dismiss anybody if you are angry, or drunk (unforgivable).
2 *Don't* issue those written warnings without *talking* directly to the would-be recipient *first*.
3 *Don't* make jokes, however mild, during the final conversation.
4 *Don't* fire people at Christmas or on New Year's Eve.
5 *Don't negotiate*. You've reached your decision – act on it.
6 *Don't* fire anybody *publicly*. Ever. It should be a discreet and relatively private affair (plus the occasional witness if necessary).
7 *Don't* get maudlin or emotional – or even too sympathetic. Mr Cool is what you need to be.

And a handful of *do's*.

1 *Do* try and have the final conversation early in the day. First thing in the morning is ideal.
2 *Do* be brief. Spare both of you too much embarrassment.
3 *Do* insist the employee leaves *that* day.

4 *Do* keep it formal. Avoid any false mateyness, e.g.:
  'This hurts me more than it's going to hurt you.'

Finally, remember this. If you are called upon to fire
somebody it means that *you* have failed a little yourself
too, especially if you hired that person in the first place.
There are times, after all, when life at the top is tough,
but hopefully, in your role of manager this most unpleasant
of duties will be perfomed very rarely.

4
The younger person as sales manager

The young person as sales manager, sometimes referred to as a 'young turk', is a fairly recent phenomenon. In the high-tech industries like computers or in the fast-shifting worlds of fashion, advertising and music it is the man or woman in his or her early thirties or even less who sits in the swivel chair and makes the big decisions. Not all of the staff will be from the same generation. Indeed, quite a few of them will be old enough to be the sales manager's father or mother. Handling this situation needs care and very considerable management skill.

In sales organisations there will invariably be a number of older colleagues who are doing a fine job, but who, for a variety of reasons, will never make sales management. They need to be recognised for what they are – *valued and experienced operators*, often with clients who are very loyal to them personally. A shrewd young manager will be careful not to disorientate the older reps by trying to force them to change too quickly or too dramatically, and should observe, *scrupulously*, the simple social courtesies like addressing them by their proper names. Older men hate being called 'Smith' by people twenty years their junior. Mr Smith, is much better. Christian names are better still, provided that is common practice in the company concerned. Older women too are sensitive to the way in which they are addressed by the young boss. Jokey references to 'aunty' or 'dearie', are uncool, sexist and patronising, and they should be painstakingly avoided.

Naturally, there will be the inevitable old soldier who trys to wrong-foot a youthful superior, and he or she should be treated firmly, but with cool civility. 'Thank you, Mr Grimes, I appreciate your advice but I do believe we should, on this occasion, talk with the client's marketing director' is infinitely preferable to, 'What? Waste our time on that dead-beat contact of yours, Grimes? You must be joking – the marketing director's the guy who makes the decisions!'

One of the cleverest young sales managers I knew always seemed to be asking advice of his older colleagues, and during these subtle exchanges was always able to interject his own message or instruction without giving offence.

Clients, too, can be spooked by a too-young sales manager suddenly arriving on their doorstep when they've grown accustomed to venerable old Freddie Wilkins with whom they play golf on a Saturday. If you need to meet a client who is a favourite of your older rep, get the rep to take you along and introduce you. Be as charming and open as you can, and *under no circumstances* upstage or pull rank on your older rep in the presence of the client. Not only will it be bad manners, it will also be bad for business.

Trying to change an older rep's method of operation is always difficult. If you send him or her away on a retraining seminar among delegates who are all fresh-faced whizz-kids, the rep will feel humiliated and demotivated. Try and pick a course that includes some older people, if you possibly can.

Older salespeople's goals and aspirations are different, too. They are less concerned about high rewards *now* and much more interested in how well funded their pension scheme is or how the company will react if they fall ill.

Clever young sales managers recognise this. Offering a sixty-year-old rep two tickets for a Bruce Springsteen concert will not be quite the treat it would be for a twenty-one-year-old. Unless the old rep likes giving his or her grandchildren a surprise.

Young sales leaders also have to find out how to handle their contemporaries, especially if they have just been promoted from the ranks. Learning to distance yourself from people you habitually hung out with at the wine bar or disco is a necessary discipline. Managers can and must *be seen* to behave in a different way from their subordinates, and it's hard to be the impartial leader when you share a hangover with a bunch of your reps and they saw you dancing on a night-club table at 3 a.m.

Young people are promoted to sales manager largely because of their *energy*, rarely because of their experience. It is this high-octane quality that boards of directors like to see fuelling the sales drive, but they are usually under no illusions about the downside risks of such an appointment. If you make it to the panelled office with the leather-topped desk and you're still trying to dry yourself behind the ears, here are a few gentle hints that may assist you in actually *staying* there.

1 Try and be yourself. Avoid the temptation of artificial maturing devices like horn-rimmed glasses and heavy pin-striped suits. You're young. Don't knock it.
2 Be even-handed in the way you deal with sales staff. Even though Tobias Grout, your fifty-eight-year-old rep in Wigan, is a bit of a whinger and you would *much* prefer to listen to Arabella Kensington, the stunning twenty-four-year-old whizz person who has doubled turnover in the SW7 district of London.
3 Learn to use or borrow the experience of others. Older

staff will be delighted to give you the benefit of their long service.

4 Don't be *too* greedy, *too* soon. Young people are always in a hurry, and many a dazzling career has spluttered out like a damp firework because of arrogance and forced growth. Forced growth is quite simply getting promoted beyond your capabilities, and the phenomenon has been dissected in countless other books on management and executive performance. Resolve to become the *best possible* sales manager before you even *think* about sales director.

5 If *you fail* (oh yes, it does happen) you'll find those people to whom you were fair and sympathetic will return the compliment as you tumble from your managerial perch. Those people to whom you were a pompous little pinhead will queue up to drive their boots into your groin. And who can blame them?

When I was nineteen years old I was commissioned as a young officer in the British Army. I remember arriving at my regiment in Austria and being introduced to my platoon sergeant, who was about double my age and fresh from active service in the Korean War. My own knowledge of *practical* soldiering and leadership would have almost filled a thimble, although I had studied theory very diligently at the Eaton Hall officer cadet school in Chester.

I had a straight choice, as the new platoon commander. I could issue instructions based on my theoretical knowledge, and the sergeant would obey – without question. Or I could ask the sergeant for his advice. Fortunately, I took the latter course and my military career got started on firm foundations. Other young subalterns who thought they knew it all took the alternative stance and simply pulled rank. I sincerely believe they lived to regret it bitterly.

There is no real substitute for experience, and the young manager must recognise this.

All the above notwithstanding, the new manager must also be prepared for a barrage of truly naff advice shovelled by people of limited ability and dubious motives. Sometimes it is not easy to distinguish the genuine from the phoney, but he or she will have to try. I was once confronted by an ageing rep, who yelled, 'I've had twenty years' experience' but in truth, I knew the poor man had really only *one year's* experience, repeated twenty times.

Finally, the young manager should recognise that the passage of time is indiscriminate and that he or she too will become a mature executive with eager puppies snapping at his or her heels. There is no special credit in being young. It is merely a passing phase, and above all, it is a time for *learning, improving and performing.*

5
Motivation, inspiration and other handy tools

You will hear the statement 'Salespeople need to be motivated' many times during your career and you will hear it so often that it will cease to hold any real meaning for you. But abused though the word is, motivation provides the key to really supercharged sales performance. First of all, let's look at the Cassell's dictionary definition of motivation: 'That which incites to action, or determines the will. Any impelling force that instigates.'

'Incitement to action' is a resonant phrase, imbued with military overtones, and is it what you, as a sales leader, are expected – indeed, *required* – to provide. Of course, motivation can take many forms, and most of them are interdependent. Here's my priority list of what *really* motivates people.

1 The right product or service. i.e. one in which the sales team *believe* and of which they are genuinely proud.
2 The right working environment. Cheerful offices. Reliable company transport (cars or vans). Sympathetic support staff in research, publicity etc.
3 Money. Don't kid yourself it isn't important. It is.
4 Recognition, career prospects, praise and self-worth.
5 Keen competition. A most effective spur to increased effort.

The newly promoted sales manager will need to study the sales team both as individuals and as a group to determine how best to motivate them. But motivation is like breathing, you have to go on doing it permanently if you don't want to curl up and die. And maintaining that impetus is one of the hardest jobs in sales management. Yes, you can juggle with sales targets, either raising them if they are too low or lowering them if they are too high. Too low? Will raising targets really act as a motivator? In many circumstances the answer is Yes.

If you, the manager, underestimate the worth or potential of your sales team they are likely to accept this value judgement and *underperform*. Getting the balance right is a tricky business. By the same token, if targets are ludicrously unattainable they will act as a *decelerator* and you will drive your sales team into a trough of despair. It's *your* hand that should be resting on the tiller, sensitive to the ebb and flow of effort that emanates from your salespeople, and you should adopt a *creative* and *flexible* approach to setting targets.

Let's return to my list of motivation priorities and look more closely at just a couple of them. Number one (the right product or service) is so obvious as to need no further elaboration. Number two (environment) is not so easy to achieve, and it falls into an area where prejudice and subjective judgement run rampant.

Some companies, wrongly in my view, take the attitude that if their sales force are out on the road most of the working week, then all they need at base is a scruffy room, sparsely furnished with other people's reject furniture and perhaps a cheap cork board on which messages are pinned. The effect this has on morale is catastrophic. A man or woman who has been in the front line representing their company deserves better than that. Comfortable, bright surroundings with decent furniture and a few plants or pictures can make a much more positive statement. In simple terms it says, '*We value you*.' That in itself is a strong motivating force.

In the fifties, when I was fresh out of the British Army and looking for work, I applied for a job with a large office equipment company whose head office was in London's West End. I was interviewed by a trendy-looking sales director with side-whiskers, a shiny mohair suit and a cheap cigar. His office was bright, almost flashy, and I remember the thick pile carpet and velvet drapes. His desk, which was the size of a medium aircraft carrier, was covered with carefully arranged executive toys: a calculator (very smart in 1955), a glass paperweight shaped like a woman's breast, a set of leather-covered letter openers in three sizes and a huge bowl of hyacinths.

I was impressed with the bold vulgarity of it all. The interview was brisk and I was further excited by the stupendous commission earnings that were clearly within my grasp if I was offered a position in the sales team.

Finally, dazzled by the prospect of untold riches, I shook hands and accepted the job. As I left, glowing with a sense of triumph, some tiny, primeval warning device inside my head told me to temper my euphoria with a touch of caution. The sales team, of which I was soon to become a part, worked not from these pristine headquarters overlooking a superbly groomed London square but from an obscure address in a much less salubrious part of town. On impulse I hailed a taxi and went directly there.

It adjoined the factory, and was no more than a suite of dingy rooms overlooking a bomb-site, a relic of World War II. As I pushed open the door marked 'reps only', I *knew* I would never actually take the job. A few salesmen were sitting around drinking tea; one of them had kicked his shoes off, and two more were playing a desultory game of cards. The general atmosphere was of lethargy, lack of interest and despair.

I told them who I was and that I'd just been offered a job. Their reaction clinched it. The turnover among salesmen was phenomenal, the much-vaunted giant commissions were no more than dangled carrots, constantly out of reach of the average rep, and any really fat account became the exclusive preserve of head office. Apparently, during the three-month probationary period, most new reps managed to open a few new accounts and as soon as they had scored, their targets or their territory were changed. If they complained, they were fired – or they quit, to be replaced by a seemingly inexhaustible stream of ex-National Service hopefuls like myself.

I was lucky to avoid joining that company. It could have soured my attitude to selling as a career, probably for ever. Treating salespeople as valued members of the company rather than expendable merchandise is an important key in maintaining motivation. The good manager will encourage the financial director or chief executive to explain company policy and the balance sheet to *all* the sales team at least once a year.

The source of much tension inside a company can often be traced back to the mild antagonism between accountants and salespeople. The good manager must not allow this rift to occur, and should seek to bring both sides to an understanding of the other's function. After all, both salespeople and accountants *need* each other. They may never *love* each other. People driving company cars around the country seldom have a lot in common with those poor employees stuck back at base. But they *can* learn to respect each other professionally.

Praising your sales team when they turn in an exceptional performance may sound pretty wet. They're *paid* to perform aren't they? They're just doing their job after all, like sanitary engineers, brain surgeons or ferret stranglers. But salespeople – and managers for that matter – *do* like *genuine* praise. Don't overdo it, though. Sobbing with gratitude and kissing the hem of your top salesperson's jacket will be considered gauche. And it will be counter-productive. But *do* recognise fine effort by saying something – and don't be afraid to drop the team the occasional memo telling them how pleased you are at some new target reached or surpassed.

The life of a sales leader, however, is not all milk and honey. Every waking moment, unfortunately, does not consist of frenzied back-slapping, lavishing praise and uncorking the champagne. Things go wrong. Targets are missed. Salespeople lose their sense of direction, and occasionally the managing director will lean hard on his sales management because of falling sales or profits.

It is a lot easier to carry out the more difficult tasks as a sales leader if you have already established a strong rapport with your team and they *know* you value them.

Some of these difficult tasks will include the *critical pep talk*, usually when sales are falling. But this too can be a minefield for the unwary. For example, you are the sales manager for ACME Laminated Nodules of Slough and sales, quite frankly, have been slipping in recent months. You *know* that the product is still good, a brand leader even, and you also know that the *potential* of your salespeople is still nowhere close to its maximum. You determine, after much thought and analysis, that a certain slackness has crept into the call-rate or the timekeeping or the sales records or the new business pitches. You decide to give the crucial pep talk. Here's what *not* to do:

1 Call the meeting at 6.30 p.m. when everybody is at a low ebb. Or even knackered.
2 Shout.

3 Use phrases like:
   'You idle heap of scum-bags!' or
   'Call yourself salespeople? You couldn't unload a half-price raft to a drowning millionaire.'
   Both these dainty exhortations I have actually heard used on a bewildered sales team!
4 Threaten hideously. Hints of redundancy or slow boiling in hot pitch do not induce confidence.
5 Pretend it's not you who is upset but higher management who are putting the squeeze on.
6 Weep or collapse whimpering over your desk because the managing director has threatened to flay the skin from your back and feed your raw, bleeding carcass to a shoal of ravening pirhana fish.
7 Claim you could do better yourself with one hand tied behind your back. You *couldn't*, you pompous twit.

What you *should* aim for is a positive approach. Express your clear disappointment certainly, but the main thrust of your little talk should be *how we can, together, get sales moving again*. Encourage debate. Maybe you'll learn something about *why* sales are falling. Be firm, particularly if you know there has been corner-cutting or lazy sales preparation. Say, 'You are capable of so much more,' and encourage the individuals in the team to examine their own particular shortcomings. *Make absolutely certain that all the necessary support services are in place.*

If sales are falling because the research department aren't providing the right brief, or because deliveries are erratic – you must shift the blame elsewhere. Be utterly *positive* that all the things the company has promised to provide *have* been provided. Little things mean a lot.

If a salesman or saleswoman has been promised a new car, or a salary rise, or a fresh set of accounts, and *management* have failed to deliver, this is a powerfully negative, demotivating force. It *will* affect performance and it will *go on* affecting performance until *you* as the manager put it right. Ignoring bad sales performance is fatal. It will not right itself; you need to take action before a hiccup becomes serious.

Just occasionally, you will identify a salesperson who has so consistently failed that you will have to remove them. This painful process is discussed in a previous chapter.

Motivation is, when you think about it, very similar to inspiration and again I am drawn to the Cassell's dictionary definition:

Inspiration The act of drawing air into the lungs, or infusing feelings, ideas etc. Supernatural influence, especially that exerted by the holy spirit on certain teachers and writers so as to impart a certain divine element to their utterances.

So if you think you're an *inspirational* sales manager, you've got a lot to live up to!

6
Talking to the board – some tips to help you avoid disaster

In most sales organisations the sales force itself is not unionised. This places a special responsibility on the shoulders of sales management, who may well have to adopt the dual roles of boss *and* shop steward. Confused? You shouldn't be; keeping a sales environment alive and kicking sometimes requires an unorthodox approach, not least of all when you are *representing the case* for the sales department to your own superiors. Let me explain just what I mean.

When a sales manager, or more frequently a sales director, is reporting on revenue performance to the board, he or she is also in a position to create a better understanding of the salesperson's role. To confine himself or herself only to the numbers, even the sacred bottom line, is shortchanging the sales department.

Even today, in these enlightened times, many corporate executives with career backgrounds in finance, law, production or engineering only vaguely appreciate the crucial nature of the *marketing* and *selling* function.

Indeed, in some production-orientated companies, the sales activity is considered to be almost peripheral. 'If we clever people *make* something' – runs the spurious argument – 'then it will just sell itself.'

These types must be told, firmly and repeatedly, that *nothing sells itself*. This is a foolish myth put about by dissident accountants who are jealous of the fun and freedom they assume all salespeople enjoy. It is a serious responsibility of the sales manager, therefore, to educate colleagues and make sure that the sales team are not misunderstood. The sales manager may also have to defend high commission earnings to colleagues who are experiencing the first twinges of envy, even hostility.

A sales leader who remains cool and persuasive can display a commitment to the old concept of the sales team as *crack troops* in the battle for profits. Sticking briefly with military metaphors, I've always compared accountants with the vital quartermaster's role in an advancing army, the research and advertising function as being the reassuring thump of artillery support and the sales force in the field being either the infantry with fixed bayonets or even the cavalry at full charge. Allusions to the field of combat are not as fanciful as you might at first suppose. A lot of marketing terminology owes its pedigree to language used in the armed forces, 'sales offensives', 'sales drives', 'attacking gaps in the market' and so on.

Now although it may be hard to bottle up your enthusiasm for the great job you believe your sales team are doing, you also have to realise that a board meeting is not the right forum for displays of explosive emotion. You *will* be closely questioned about the way you run the department and you must guard against being touchy, or over-sensitive. State your case, by all means, but never try to bamboozle or deceive with lame excuses for bad performance. If sales are *down*, your job is to identify *why* they are down and then concentrate on *solutions*. Indeed, as a general rule, boards of directors much prefer sales managers who offer solutions rather than painstakingly elaborate analyses of failure.

It is also perhaps stating the obvious to say that you should prepare your presentation to the board with as much care as you would if they were a major client. *But be brief*. Nothing irritates a board room full of busy directors more than a garrulous young sales manager. *Be positive. Don't waffle*. Resolve to go away after the meeting and *find* the answer. And be *sure* you give it to them next time round. Not knowing once is just about acceptable. Not knowing twice begins to sound like carelessness. Not knowing three times suggests you might be better off peeling grapes for a living instead.

If you are required to submit a written report *before* a board meeting, don't fall into the trap of making it almost as long as a Harold Robbins novel. Bulky submissions have an extraordinary effect on corporate executives – they either,

(A) don't get read *at all*

    or

(B) get read grudgingly

Those who haven't read them feel disadvantaged and obliged to ask elaborate questions to mask their ignorance. This irritates those who *have* read them, and they will have identified at least one flaw or serious mistake in your submission and will pounce on it with the savagery of a man-eating Bengal tiger.

Most executives know that a good idea can be stated verbally *in less than five minutes*. I've seen genuinely brilliant propositions die from slow suffocation because the sales manager overdid the background leading up to the pitch, or tabled too much unnecessary data in his leather-bound, impressively embossed presentation.

Don't ask for more than *one* favour or concession at a single board meeting. Directors are custodians of the shareholders' funds, remember, and if a young sales manager's vocabulary is too littered with 'I wants' – especially if they cost money – he or she will experience the sharp and salutary sting of a bloody nose.

Timing is vital too – knowing *when* to ask for that investment approval in a new computer system. Just after the financial director has announced dividends ought to be cut by 75 per cent is *not* an auspicious moment for you to leap up in your beautifully cut Austin Reed suit and, smiling winsomely, suggest a sales conference in Tangier. Boards of directors are, of course, individuals, but *as a board* they can develop *group moods* or *collective reactions*. A shrewd sales manager must learn to read these moods and react accordingly. Here's a brief summary of do's and don'ts if your first meeting with the board is still to come.

Do's	*Don't's*
Do be brief.	*Don't* oversell.
	Don't submit too long a report.
Do be positive.	*Don't* ask for more than one favour or concession at a time.
Do take the opportunity to enhance the image of the sales team.	*Don't* deal in problems, only solutions.
Do prepare in advance.	*Don't* busk. If you don't know the answer, say so.
Do be interesting.	*Don't* promise what you can't deliver.

And if after your first meeting you haven't got exactly what it was you were seeking, or even if you emerge from the inner sanctum feeling as if your brain has been squeezed through a mangle (a common syndrome after long board meetings), you must never return to the sales department full of grumbles and complaints about 'them'. As a manager you have to maintain a most delicate balancing trick between your own subordinates and your own superiors.

It is poor management practice to blame your boss for every mistake or set-back. Your own staff will become sceptical very quickly, knowing you are attempting to throw a smoke-screen around your own inadequacies. It is even worse management practice to bad-mouth your own department to your superiors if you happen to be under attack or in a tight corner. Remember, there are no inefficient salespeople without inefficient managers. So if you slag off those in your charge, the board will draw their own conclusions – and they won't be cosy.

Try to absorb the rhythm and the atmosphere of your own company's *meeting style*. Not everybody runs a formal horn-rimmed sort of meeting with neatly typed minutes and agendas. Many companies prefer the more relaxed approach with the minimum of formality. As a young manager, don't go against the grain. Go with the flow.

And finally, do *listen*. Other people have important things to say besides you – hard as that might be to accept. You should aim to leave every meeting having *learnt at least one fact about your company*. If you do this, you will succeed. If you only go to meetings to hear the sound of your own voice, you won't succeed. The choice is yours.

7
Matchmaking, people-watching, oil, water, chalk and cheese

Abracadabra, you're in the boss's chair. Just think of all those marvellous changes you intend to make. It will be as if a white tornado hit the sales department, sweeping all before it to a new plateau of prosperity, profit and perpetual sunshine. If you really think like that, perhaps you should become a gravedigger in Khartoum, because your chances of success will be distinctly better. Magic wands you leave behind at school. The real world needs managers who can identify problems and solve them with thought and action. And nothing worthwhile is ever that easy.

One of the most important tasks confronting a sales manager is the allocation of human resources, or to put it a little more crudely – which rep handles which client and how often should they be changed around? This is critical because *buying is largely an emotional response* and a selling organisation needs to acknowledge this fact. Is that a ludicrous statement? Not at all. Nearly all decisions to buy are triggered by an emotional response and later justified by *post-emotional rationalisation*. Why do you buy a new car? Is the old one really clapped out? Why do you want that shiny electric typewriter for your secretary? Your letters still got typed on the old one, didn't they? In fact you purchase the new car or the new office toy because it is a symbol of status or a statement to the world about *you* and how you *want* to be perceived. A new, bigger house with a pool? It's the kind of property that mirrors the image you want others to think is the real, successful you.

So, matching your salesmen and your saleswomen to the appropriate client can assist in this emotional mix. Let's take a very simple example.

Client X is a polished, urbane, public-school-educated man with a very high opinion of himself and the social level at which he operates. You need to allocate a representative to service his business and you have two people on your team whom you can choose.

Representative A is a tough, no-nonsense cockney who has demonstrated great skill in tackling new accounts and has turned in spectacular sales figures in one of your toughest territories. But he likes a couple of pints and a game of darts after work and he *is* rather fond of pale blue suits and hand-painted neckties.

Representative B is a smooth, public-school-educated – I don't really have to go on, do I? It's a pretty obvious choice. Even an idiot sales manager would get that one right. OK. How about this example:-

Client Y is a total bastard. Rude, difficult, quick-tempered, really hates salespeople but he *does* spend serious money with your company, good old ACME Laminated Nodules of Slough. He also plays golf – not very well, but often.

Representative C is a tough guy too. Skin like a rhinoceros and capable of dishing it out with the best of them. He's a skilled negotiator even though he has a bit of a short fuse. And he plays an excellent game of golf.

Representative D is mild, soft-spoken and rather sensitive. She doesn't know a golf club from a stick of rhubarb, but she is persuasive, in a quiet, sincere sort of way.

Another easy choice Mr Sales Manager? Think about it. Maybe you should match tough with tough. Let them slug it out, and watch the sparks fly. On the other hand wouldn't Ms Mild (Representative D) be a clever foil for bombastic Client Y? Men who shout a lot soon stop if their audience seems impervious to the display of histrionics. And what about golf? Rep C, who wields a nifty iron might thrash the client and further exacerbate an already explosive ego. Rep D, however, will be in no such danger. There is no simple, obvious solution, but it is this kind of dilemma, involving the allocation of human resources, that will tax even the most experienced sales manager's ingenuity.

Another area that needs regular fine tuning is what I describe as the 'familiarity syndrome' or more crudely, 'the decay factor'. When a salesman or saleswoman has handled the same group of accounts for a long time, certain benefits do emerge. Knowledge of the clients' needs, an understanding of their business objectives, how soon they pay their bills, what their rate of growth might be, what their hobbies and vices are and so forth. All useful ammunition for a dedicated and conscientious salesperson.

But over-familiarity can often lead to laziness and the confusion of priorities. Salespeople who are *too* cosy with their clients will lose their cutting edge and take the easy route. 'I won't push old Joe to increase his order this month because, well – he's a *mate* really and we do use the same pub at weekends.' The 'decay factor' sets in and before long the value of that client declines – or at best remains virtually static. A new salesperson, properly matched to this client and introduced with subtlety and care, will frequently produce *more business* and *bigger orders* than the previous representative.

This is not to say that I am recommending change for change's sake. That would be foolish. What is important is to watch for the tell-tale signs, and ask yourself regularly, Is my sales team properly mixed and matched?

While on the subject of mixing, most sales teams these days are unisex, and deciding which client should be allocated the stunning redhead with legs that go on forever is no easy task. Neither is deciding which of your female clients should be introduced to Garth Bicep, the blond Adonis who makes Sylvester Stallone look like a stick insect. Be careful. Some men are intimidated by pretty women. Others go all peculiar and try a quick lunge. One thing is certain, if it goes wrong out there in that jungle called the sales territory, it's *your* backside that the managing director will roast over an open fire – and don't you forget it!

8
Handling power – now you've got some, what to do with it

The word 'power' conjures up emotive images and it is perhaps one of the goals most sought after by groups and by individuals in our society today. Even those who have acquired great wealth and all the creature comforts it normally provides, still hanker after power. Clearly, power is assumed to be a benefit to those who seek it, and popular literature frequently reminds us that it is a greater aphrodisiac than mere success.

When a salesman or saleswoman moves from a position of *receiving* orders into a position where he or she *issues* orders, a mantle of power descends upon their shoulders, even if the role assumed is that of sales supervisor with, say, only three reps reporting upwards.

No matter how limited the power attained, it requires a fundamental change in the attitude of the person who now wields it. Power was defined by the German sociologist Weber, as 'the possibility of imposing one's will upon the behaviour of other persons'. Now the ability to impose one's will on others is a dangerous privilege and, curiously enough, there are as many abuses of power among those who wield very little of it as there are among great men who hold sway over vast empires or even nation states.

We have all encountered the petty officials who over-exercise the limited authority they have been granted. The over-zealous traffic warden, the vindictive Customs officer, the pedantic Social Security clerk. We accuse them of being 'little Hitlers', 'drunk with power', or even occasionally, 'power-mad'.

Clearly power is a highly destructive force, as much to those who have it as to those upon whom it is exercised. So if you are about to trade in your battered old rep's briefcase for the heady atmosphere of a manager's job, you ought to sit down and ask yourself these questions:

Do I want power because,

1 It will help me get things done?
2 I relish the mere prospect of it, even as an abstraction?
3 I enjoy giving orders?
4 It will make me important, enhance my self-esteem?
5 It will enable me to achieve greater financial rewards?
6 Others are weak and need powerful leadership?

If you are drawn irrevocably to answers 3, 4 or 6, beware – you could have the makings of a little tyrant. If, on the other hand, you favour answers 1 and 5, then your attitude is healthy. As for answer 2, that's pretty neutral, and the contemplation of power is, after all, part of most people's harmless day-dreams.

Sales managers should seek power *only* to get things done and to obtain rewards, not just for themselves, but for those who are now reporting to them. Without the desire for benefits or rewards, there will be no motivation. Power brings with it a phantom twin called responsibility. I describe it as a phantom because many fail to recognise it even though it is there, joined to power by an invisible umbilical cord.

Those who are familiar with the exercise of power also know that it is in human nature to resist it, to set up an opposing force to it. This is especially true in western democracies, where the tradition is to question authority, debate decisions openly and criticise elected leaders.

Salespeople, by their very nature, resent being given auto-cratic commands from on high and will use all kinds of stratagems to retaliate against a tyrannical boss.

If you were serious about only wanting power in order to get things done, then you will know already that persuasion is much more effective than brute force. This is not to say that you should be a weak, vacillating manager. Your power base gives you the right to make decisions and to see that they are properly executed. The difference between a shrewd manager and a dumb one, however, is the *way in which his power is wielded*:

'I really think we ought to improve the daily call rate in your section, David. The average across the team is six, and your people are only delivering four. I'd like to see an improvement on next month's call sheets, please' is strong and unequivocal, and better than:

'If you don't pull six calls a day in your section, heads will roll. So do it.'

The first method establishes the manager's priorities and makes them quite plain. He wants six calls a day. This is the norm, and all he is asking is for this particular section to perform *at par* with their colleagues. It's fair, it's reasonable, and it's hard to resist. The second method will cause hackles to rise and defensive mechanisms to snap into play. The wretched section leader David will find his team offering excuses why they can't deliver six calls a day in order to resist the raw power they sense is being exercised on them.

The most awesome concept of power is that which is known to be there *but is never used*. The nuclear arms race is perhaps too grotesque an example but it is nevertheless a display of muted power that we all hope will never be utilised. The best boss is the one who can emanate powerful vibrations without needing to bully, cajole or scream at his subordinates. Of course, it is not always easy to keep your cool when you are under pressure as a manager – but you should always set out to make this your goal. Possessing power and using it sparingly *enhances the concept of your power* rather than diminishes it.

The power-crazy manager who issues a stream of staccato commands, fires people indiscriminately and bulldozes his way forward is using up all his ammunition too soon. What shots will he have left in the breach when a *real* crisis flares up?

Powerful men and women appear relaxed and confident during those moments when they are actually exercising power. It's the subtle hint of untapped strength that creates the best impression. With a speed limit of 70 m.p.h. in this country, why do men still buy Jaguars and Mercedes and Ferraris? In city traffic, nobody can really steal much of an advantage but the *potentially powerful* vehicle exudes a *promise of performance* that is in itself a statement of superiority. You don't need to hurl your Mercedes along the motorway at 130 m.p.h. to demonstrate it's got poke – people know, just by looking at it.

It's not all that different with managers. If you behave as if there is much more untapped horsepower under *your* bonnet than you are prepared to show – *your subordinates will believe it*.

The power wielded in business corporations is very different to that which exists in a military hierarchy. The latter is based upon a rigid concept of disciplines where the issue and acceptance of orders is almost second nature. 'Theirs not to reason why, theirs but to do and die.' Men who have learnt to exercise power in the armed forces often fail when they make the transition to private business. Unlike the army, the navy, or the air force, a whole apparatus of resistance is in place to act as a counterbalance to the power of the executive. The most obvious of these is the trade union movement. In my experience, good officers don't usually make good managers, although there are spectacular exceptions.

Finally, one of the ways to *increase* your inventory of power, your untapped resources of the stuff, is quite simply to be successful. The more successful you become, the more power people will assume you have – and not only that, you'll only need to use a fraction of it. Just like a Ferrari throbbing with menace at the traffic lights!

So remind yourself, the day you are promoted to manager, you will exercise your power as if it were a precious resource, and you will only use it to fulfil that honourable trinity of aims: to get things done, to improve the rewards for you and your subordinates, and to make your organisation more successful.

As for the rest, leave that to Adolf Hitler and the traffic warden who hung around outside the crematorium waiting to give the funeral cars a parking ticket.

9
Gossip – a sales manager's hotline to the truth, or a bum steer?

Put a group of people together in a working environment, particularly if the sexes are mixed, and one of the things that can be *positively guaranteed* to emerge is that most tantalising of all commodities, gossip.

Hopefully, other things will emerge too – like performance and growth and success – but they will ebb and flow like the tide, whereas gossip will keep on bubbling to the surface with the persistence of an inexhaustible volcano. So what? Why should an aspiring sales manager pay the smallest attention to such a trivial, even worthless activity? OK, let's see what the dictionary definition of the word is: 'Casual and idle chat. A conversation involving malicious chatter or rumours about other people.' Sounds even worse, doesn't it, and a far cry from those sales targets, marketing analyses and five-year-growth plans.

But an experienced manager knows that salespeople are probably among the most volatile folk in the company and like nothing better than a touch of gossip. An old colleague of mine, now retired, once said he knew how a particular policy directive he had issued was *really* received by the sales team after he had listened to the tea lady summing up staff reaction as she poured out his mid-morning cup of Earl Grey. The tea lady's nattering was in fact a distillation of all the vibrations she had absorbed from staff as she did her daily rounds. She knew if the boys and girls on the sales floor were happy or unhappy about any particular issue because they would unload their true feelings in front of her in a clearly unexpurgated form.

I am bound to say that I would not recommend such a method of gathering intelligence as it smacks of tittle-tattle, or even espionage, but the point remains valid – gossip can sometimes reflect the feelings of a group far more accurately than a formal question-and-answer session. The problem is, what gossip to believe and what to dismiss as fantasy. I have an unproven theory about this. Let me try it out for size.

If, as a manager, you accidentally overhear gossip, i.e. *conversations you are not supposed to be party to,* you must ignore them. Even if the chatter is about *you,* and furthermore, what is being said is mildly unflattering. Always remember that it is *quite natural* for staff to grumble occasionally about the boss. Haven't you? So grit your teeth and banish it from your mind. Unless of course you overhear those two reps from Barnsley planning to tar and feather you in the same barrel as Reggie Fudgebucket the chief accountant. If you seize upon the occasional staff indiscretion in the corridor and blow it out of all proportion, you will soon acquire the reputation of Attila the Hun – and much worse, people will only gossip *even more furtively.*

If, on the other hand, your secretary or one of your trusted lieutenants tells you of a persistent rumour or strength of feeling in the department, you can be almost certain that the message, although filtering through a third person, is *ultimately intended for your ears.*

In my experience, this method of floating suggestions or objections through an aide or secretary has a time-honoured pedigree. If you choose to ignore the information – or even if you act on it – faces can be saved, and there is no risk of a one-to-one confrontation. The downside risks of using this method to check the tempera-

ture of your department are, however, rather grave –
especially if your source is a known carrier of malicious
trivia. So be as certain as you can that your secretary, for
example, is a mature and responsible person with no
obvious axe to grind. I have had my card marked on many
occasions by a very shrewd PA who knew just what to pass
on to me – and perhaps much more important than that,
what *not* to.

Clearly the grapevine method of information-gathering
is no substitute for open meetings and frank exchanges
between manager and sales staff, but it would be a mistake
to dismiss it altogether.

If a rumour of disturbing proportions is floating around
the office, and it reaches you via an acceptable source, e.g.
your secretary or deputy, you must then make a decision
as to whether to confirm or deny it *officially*. And you must
make that decision *quickly*.

For example, at the high-tech offices of Laminated
Nodules of Slough, your secretary tells you of a strong
rumour circulating about drastic changes in the
commission scale – the story, which is hot in the canteen,
is that you, the sales manager, have agreed with your
managing director to *slash* commissions by 30 per cent
because of a squeeze on profits.

Now, you have two courses of action, depending on the
status of the rumour. If the rumour is false – and so many
of them are – you should call an *immediate meeting* of all
your staff and put the record straight. And do it calmly.
There's no need for arm-waving and expressions of shock
horror or pain.

If, to your genuine shock, horror and pain, the rumour
is true – and you have hatched a plan to screw the earnings
of your sales team – you'd better call that meeting anyway,
and you'd also better have a damn good reason for having
allowed the bad news to leak out. If you *have* been talking

it over with the MD and were overheard, you *must apologise* and make the best of a very poor job.

How do you deal with gossip which is of a personal or private nature – e.g. Garth Bicep, the blond Adonis in sales, is having it off with Arabella Kensington *every night* on the way home in the back of his Vauxhall Cavalier,

or

Sid Fruitcake in accounts dresses up in Girl Guide's uniform at weekends and is partial to light whipping at an establishment in the Edgware Road

or even

The managing director's wife is a paid-up member of the Nazi Party (Slough branch), and has plans to invade Czechoslavakia next Tuesday?

Here's what you do if such gossip reaches your ears. Nothing. Absolutely nothing.

However, let us suppose that young Garth Bicep's proclivities include pleasuring lovely Arabella Kensington in the computer room during working hours behind the high-speed printer! Then you have a cause for legitimate concern. But for God's sake be careful – tackling people on delicate subjects needs special skill and you have to be absolutely certain that *your facts are unimpeachable*. If in doubt, shut up.

Sometimes a manager can utilise the grapevine of gossip himself, by floating an unusual suggestion through the usual channels and waiting for feedback. More seriously, the tribal instincts of a sales team can often flag the manager about a single colleague who has problems or is underperforming by means of the unofficial grapevine.

Nevertheless, considerable pitfalls do exist, and it bears repeating that gossip is no substitute for an open style of dialogue between staff and managers. So keep your ears pricked; try and hire a secretary who is honest and well respected by your staff as well as you; ignore what you weren't intended to hear, and act on what was *deliberately* leaked; and only intervene on private matters if your judgement tells you the problem will adversely affect your business performance.

Last word on gossip from Warren Beatty, the film actor with a reputation as a modern-day Lothario. 'If all the gossip about my sex life were true' – he is reported to have said – 'then I wouldn't be giving this press conference, I'd be on a laboratory shelf pickled in a jar.'

10
How to behave halfway up the ladder of success

Why only halfway? What about the top and bottom rungs?

Because halfway is where the rungs are slippery and where everybody else above and below is staring at you in the fervent hope that you will fall off like a sack of damp artichokes.

People at the very top, you may have noticed, can behave in an appalling manner and get away with it, whereas those poor bastards at the bottom – well, nobody expects anything from them anyway.

A peer of the realm will readily find apologists for his boorish, clumsy social habits who will excuse them as eccentricities – 'Lord Clenchwarton's a real card. Did you see him pouring custard over that waiter's shoe?' Or, 'Sir Ranulph Snufftruscket's in a sporty mood – he's just locked his secretary in the stationery cupboard with a live ferret.'

I've known a multi-millionaire who still rolls his own cigarettes and changes his socks once a week. With an aspiring person at midpoint in his or her career, such quirks would be positively damaging. For a salesperson they could be terminal. At the bottom end of the scale, fag-rolling and rotting socks may be a repulsive but *acceptable* feature of the boilerman's behaviour. Poor old Bert's life is pretty unhappy anyway. Best to ignore it really. Can't impose bourgeois standards on the British working man.

Salt of the earth. He'll resent being patronised. And so on and so forth.

But for you in mid-career, upwardly mobile, with the stupendous mortgage and spouse who is just getting the taste of Taittinger '64, you, my friend, have got to watch your P's and Q's. The balancing trick you have to perform on those middle rungs is precarious in the extreme. To begin with, you've got to be noticed. It's no good thundering along in the centre of the herd, obscured by the dust of their pounding hooves. (And *don't* ask me how this trick is performed in the middle of a metaphor about ladders!)

So. You must be conspicuous. But not so way-out as to cast doubts in the minds of your superiors, who might suspect they have a lunatic lurking in the sales department.

Your visibility or high-profile style can only be achieved by work-related behaviour. Any oddities of dress or manner must have some relevance, however tenuous, with your job specification.

Your obsession with tennis, for example, and your wearing of the bright orange club tie can be quietly justified by letting it be known that your firm's major customer is a Wimbledon fanatic who sleeps with a picture of Martina Navratilova under his pillow.

An obsessive interest in opera is quite acceptable too. It sets you above the mob whose idea of culture is an LP of Max Bygraves singing a medley of hits from the 1950s. Warbling bits from *La Traviata* during sales meetings, however, is not a good idea.

Avoid becoming a car fanatic. Many a promising mid-career in sales has floundered because of a deadly and overwhelming interest in sports cars, exhaust systems and wire wheels. Don't ask me why such a hobby causes top management to cringe – it may remain a mystery until the end of time.

We are, of course, talking about *extreme* manifestations of enthusiasm. Collecting vintage cars is fine. Coming into the office with black grease embedded under the fingernails and your neck in plaster due to whiplash on the Norbiton Amateur Grand Prix circuit is *not* fine.

Well, is there any rule of thumb as far as all this is concerned?

How do you get noticed on those middle rungs without incurring the wrath of those above and the contempt of those below?

To begin with, you should be careful not to poach your superior's territory. If you work for a sales director who is conspicuously proud of her golf handicap, it ill behoves you – callow youth that you are – to whip the daylights out of her when she invites you to play with her at Sunningdale.

And then boast about it in the office.

If your boss fancies himself as a keep-fit fanatic and runs up two flights of stairs each day to impress the girls in the office, don't flash past him with an impish grin or offer to carry his briefcase.

If, on the other hand, he believes he is the combined reincarnation of Rudolph Valentino, Errol Flynn and Richard Burton, beware of sneaking a cuddle with his secretary behind his back. Or his wife, for that matter. Unless the lady is *uncommonly* plain and stout to the point of obesity. Such wives are cuddle-starved and a discreet hug from you may – just – enhance your career . . . 'Oh John, that *thoughtful* young salesman you have in the department – Blenkinsop, I think his name is. *So* considerate. I bet he's *very* persuasive.'

However, being discovered writhing naked on the boardroom table with the boss's lady, whether she be his wife, mistress, secretary or mother, is not a sound tactic.

You can, however, be exposed locked in a lustful

embrace with his daughter *only* if you plan to marry her. And if you're a fella, try and avoid pouncing on the boss's son.

The rules for women are the same – but in reverse!

Behaviour patterns are most likely to be exposed and commented upon at certain set-piece functions like the company dance or in the restaurant. For the man or woman in mid-career who still throbs with ambition, here's a 'do' and 'don't' list for these two situations.

Remember, you *want* to be noticed and looked upon as a special person with potential but at the same time you *don't* want to be conspicuous for the *wrong* reasons. It's a hell of a tightrope on the middle rung of the ladder amongst that thundering herd. (A new world record for mixed metaphors will be attempted later on in this book!)

First of all, that hideous quicksand – the company party.

Don'ts

Don't get drunk. Even slightly.

Don't grope your superiors. Or even your juniors.

Don't forget your underarm deodorant.

Don't stay with your cronies all evening.

Don't overeat.

Don't be the last to leave. Don't be the first, either.

Don't ignore the tea-lady, the janitor, the post boy.

Don't get dragged into political arguments.

Do's

Do stay sober and cheerful.

Do dance with as many people as time allows.

Do dress immaculately. And I mean – *take trouble*.

Do circulate.

Do eat sparingly.

Do thank the boss/host before leaving.

Do dance *well*. (If you can't, don't dance at all. Your bad leg is playing you up, isn't it?)

Do listen to people for a change.

59

Don't yawn during the chairman's address.

Do thank the waiter/chef as you leave.

Don't wear a funny paper hat for more than ten minutes.

Do try and be seen in keen conversation with a senior member of the accounts department.

Don't enter any competition which involves being blindfolded or showing your knee-caps.

Do regularly check how you look during the course of the evening. Fragments of iced cake on the nose are a killer.

Don't sing along with the band.

In the restaurant, if the boss is buying:

Don'ts

Do's

Don't overeat or drink. Moderation, baby, is your bag.

Do be punctual.

Don't belch.

Do chew with your mouth shut.

Don't pick any dish you can't finish.

Do avoid garlic.

Don't disagree with the choice wine – even if it's Congolese Beaujolais.

Do compliment their choice of restaurant, wine, etc.

Don't have a pudding.

Do try and look relaxed, even if it's your first time at the Ritz.

Don't lick your knife.

Do answer all the boss's questions after you've finished swallowing.

Don't try and see the bill.

Do go to the loo before the meal starts.

60

So watch your step and keep climbing that ladder. If you reach for the stars you may not actually touch them – but you will have much more fun trying than if you lurk on the bottom rung, scratching around in the compost.

11
Power lunching and the pitfalls of gluttony

A curious thing, the business lunch. It takes place daily in the western world on a regular and increasing scale. Countless tons of shrimp cocktails are prepared and eaten every twenty-four hours in such quantity as would suggest the oceans may soon run dry of the little creatures.

An equally daunting if marginally more trivial piece of information is that if all the fillet steaks chewed and ingested in all the London restaurants for one year were laid end to end you could carpet Blenheim Palace in one-inch thick red meat with a few yards left over to store in the freezer. Not as they say, a very appealing prospect. Especially if you're a vegetarian or a live bull.

The purpose of this chapter, however, is not to reveal a sheaf of awe-inspiring statistics about the length, depth, width or consistency of food consumed at a typical business lunch – however fascinating and predictable to the nutritionist. Instead we shall try to examine the subtle art of power lunching.

It is, of course, never 'just a meal'. The business lunch is a tribal ritual imbued with magic and pockmarked with pitfalls for the unwary. To begin with, the person who is paying for lunch starts off in the pole position. It is he or she who can select the restaurant, the location of the table (now more important than even the food!) and display a casually modest knowledge of the wine list. The 'lunchee' as we shall now henceforth describe him or her is at a clear disadvantage. The lunchee can in extreme circumstances ask for the restaurant chosen to be changed – but the reasons, even for an important client, must be plausible. 'Because I am allergic to Chinese food' is OK. 'Because I'm taking my lover there tonight' is less so. Although, come to think of it, that's not such a bad idea after all. However, let's deal with the person who is actually footing the bill for the power-lunch. If they wish to score high marks and impress their 'lunchee' here are a few simple ground rules.

1 Always pick a restaurant where you are well known. (Save experimental new ones for your spouse or friends.)

2 Try to indicate which table you prefer. Best tables should command a view of the whole restaurant. Being seen, contrary to all this guff about discreet private rooms, is the important thing.

3 Warn the head waiter if your lunchee is difficult, e.g. a drunk (the waiter will know to be light on the gin and heavy on the tonic), or a food faddist. Also tell the manager if your lunchee is *really* important to you. Devise a scale of 1–5 and award a rating to each person you lunch – 1 is a big wheel.

4 Rehearse your knowledge of the menu beforehand so that if the lunchee asks you what you recommend you can respond smoothly without blurting out something fatuous like, 'Er – the fish is usually good!'

5 If your knowledge of wine is like most people's, i.e. strictly limited, don't try and come on like the Duc de St Tropez and start prattling about 'cheeky young Chablis with a hint of fruitiness' or 'deep full-bodied clarets from a little vineyard on the south-eastern slopes of an old Saracen burial mound'. The

chances are that your guest will be the son of the
sommelier at Le Gavroche and he will instantly
categorise you as a pretentious little prat.

6 Do stick to a wine that you have tried before and
genuinely enjoyed. The wine waiter will help you,
especially if you don't try and upstage him.

7 Food. Now this may seem strange but at a power
lunch the host should eat sparingly and avoid those
dishes which need excessive chewing or those which
can induce hiccups or temporary blindness – like
vindaloo curry. Nouvelle cuisine is ideal – it's pretty
to look at and can be consumed with scarcely an
interruption to your flow of conversation.

8 The power luncher never eats puddings or drinks
liqueurs. Not even if the lunchee forks down a Black
Forest gâteau the size of a boxing glove and follows
it by two double Rémy Martins.

9 The power luncher *must* be seen by other important
people as they enter or leave the restaurant. But be
careful not to overdo it. Nodding and smiling at
Michael Caine, Henry Kissinger and Princess
Margaret is fine. Leaping up and pumping the hand
of Bruce Forsyth or Joseph Mengele's hairdresser
is considered gauche.

10 The power luncher is not afraid to launch straight
into business chat early on in the meal. Too much
valuable time is wasted at business lunches in bone-
numbing small talk. I mean, do you really give a toss
about rotten golf handicaps or adventures at the
Neasden branch of Weightwatchers? Of course you
don't. Smile knowingly and say something like: 'I
know your time is valuable so I know you won't
mind me kicking straight off into the business.' No
lunchee has ever been known to object to this ploy,
and it usually stems any further grisly anecdotes about

children's teeth braces or that row with the local gas board.

11 The power lunch should be relatively short. Experienced practitioners never sit around in an empty restaurant while waiters stack tables or hover menacingly with those special glassy smiles they reserve for gourmets who won't go home even though it's now 3.15.

12 Another invaluable tip if, like me, you are mildly accident prone with food, always make sure you cover yourself with a snowy white napkin. It is hard to maintain the initiative if a strand of spaghetti is sliding down your shirt front or you drop a perfectly rounded button mushroom on to your two-hundred-quid dress. I once tried to pitch a client with a frayed asparagus tip clinging to my breast pocket. I was not successful.

13 If you are well known at the restaurant of your choice it sometimes pays to keep a copy of their current menu at your office – particularly if the lunchee is coming there first. It can be both impressive and time-saving if your secretary phones over your choice of food while you're in the taxi – and it's a nice touch to have your starters actually on the table when you arrive.

14 Try and select a restaurant that suits the *lunchee's* own style. Not everybody feels comfortable in the Ritz – or even San Lorenzo. Think about it, and choose accordingly. It's still possible to power lunch every day and remain slim, sober and successful.

Finally, here is a random list of just a few restaurants in London and elsewhere at which power lunching at its most potent can be observed by the dedicated student with either a fistful of money or a wallet lined with credit cards.

Power-lunching Venues London

The Ritz
Langan's Brasserie
A l'Ecu de France
Cecconi's
Savoy Grill
The Connaught
The White Tower
L'Escargot
Inigo Jones
Le Gavroche

Power-lunching Venues Elsewhere

Maxims (Paris)
Lutèce (New York)
The Gritti Palace (Venice)
The Midland Hotel (Manchester)
The Waterside Inn (Bray)
The Bel-Air Hotel (Los Angeles)
Maxims (Tokyo)
1789 (Georgetown, Washington)

The lists, needless to say, are incomplete; there are dozens you could add, according to your own taste.

12
The sales conference – Revivalist meeting or Nuremburg rally?

Ask ten salesmen from the same company what benefits they obtain from their annual sales conference and you'll probably receive ten quite different replies.

Not all of them will necessarily fit in with the company's own perception of what the conference is about either.

Confused? You needn't be. Sales conferences serve a multiplicity of objectives, as we shall examine in this chapter, and pretty well all of them are beneficial to employers and employed alike.

To begin with, salesmen and saleswomen are gregarious. They respond positively to other people. Their tribal instincts are strong and there is something primitive and tribal about putting a few dozen salespeople under the same roof for two or three days, whether they are insurance reps or commercial travellers in crematorium accessories.

Let's start by listing the most common objectives of the typical sales conference.

To review the past year's performance
To discuss targets for the future
To present new research findings about products and
    markets
To present sales policy and explain company philosophy
To develop 'in-house' training sessions
To rally enthusiasm

To develop team spirit and corporate loyalty
To improve the commercial education of the sales team
To say a corporate thank-you for another year of hard
   work

All these, or variations of them, are valid objectives for any company to pursue. In my experience the sales conference should be invested with a sense of occasion. It must be set up and planned as an important and vital part of the company's activity. The infrastructure must be sound: a good venue, up-to-date visual and audio equipment, comfortable seats, excellent communications.

If possible, take the sales team away from base – it's never very inspiring to conduct a morale-boosting event on the same old company premises.

Pick an exotic location – as exotic as your budget will allow. Plan well ahead, and I do mean well ahead. My PA starts thinking about next year's conference a week after we get back from this year's.

People must look forward to the event with special anticipation and back on it with affection.

Establish a programme that will achieve all your objectives and, above all else, make it an occasion for involvement and full participation.

Sales directors who hog the limelight at the annual conference will only succeed in boring or alienating their audience. Set specific tasks and require as many people as possible to talk at the conference. Let them have a budget and the support of your research department to help them prepare their act.

Encourage role reversal. Let the salesperson be the customer and ask questions of his or her colleagues.

Inject the proceedings with a sense of competition. Run a points system for the best presentation. Give prizes.

Good ones – not vouchers for a night-school course in basket weaving.

Insist on plenty of open-forum discussions. Nourish good debate. Don't stifle the occasional contrary opinion or way-out point of view.

Make the schedule tight. By that I mean start early. Limit lunch to one hour at the most. Avoid alcohol, or at least keep it to an absolute minimum. Serve a light luncheon. People nod off in the afternoon with half a bottle of Chablis sloshing around inside their stomachs. Or a pound and a half of steak and kidney pie.

Make sure your guest presenter, if you have one, is good on his or her feet and not a stultifying wally who can't speak impressively in public.

If sales management are presenting information – e.g. price changes, information about the competition, new targets, new product developments – make absolutely certain that it is well documented so that salespeople have something to refer to after the conference. Avoid mucky, cheaply copied loose sheets of data.

Make up a glossy brochure. Put the company logo on the front. This is a big occasion, remember.

Pay particular heed to the social programme. If you throw a dinner on the last night make it special. Avoid prawn cocktail, steak and chips, and cheap plonk. Make it a meal people will talk about with fond recollection.

If you are planning the conference abroad, be sure it's a city or resort you know will be successful. Leave nothing to chance. Either go yourself or send a trusted aide in advance to check accommodation, facilities, acoustics, menus, wines, transport arrangements.

Things must go smoothly, even in a place like Gozo, the small sister island of Malta where I once ran a conference. It was a considerable success, but the splendid locals do have a somewhat laconic approach to commercial affairs. I once asked a native of Gozo what the Maltese word for mañana was. 'We have no equivalent word that conveys the same sense of urgency,' he replied.

Always mistrust travel agents who claim to know all the ropes. There is no substitute for going and looking for yourself. Drive a hard bargain. If you're flying a few dozen people into a fine resort out of season (and you will choose out of season, won't you?) then you are providing the hotel with an unexpected bonus. Don't pay published rates. Hustle for a discount.

Once there, at the conference venue, do allow at least one free evening or half-day for people to sight-see or do their own thing. Nothing is more frustrating, or incidentally counter-productive, than having two hundred salespeople in Pisa and never letting them visit the leaning tower.

If your numbers are small enough, try and keep them together as a group, but without being too heavy-handed. I have found that the most fun and the most value my own sales team have derived from a conference has been when we have voluntarily done things together.

There are some other things that sales people do together, especially when the sexes are mixed, over which a discreet veil should be drawn. A sales director has no business in commenting on the morals of his staff, unless and until they adversely affect sales performance!

Try wherever possible to capitalise on any presentations that have been given at the conference. For example, if a junior salesman or saleswoman has been asked to research and prepare a proposal for a particular market, and on the day it really clicks, even in front of colleagues, make sure the presentation is given 'live' to a real customer when you get back to base.

Don't let good new ideas go cold. If one of the team

comes up with a great concept, it's up to everybody to see that the idea becomes reality.

A word about dress. Most of the year your average salesperson is expected to look businesslike, wear a suit, a tie, or in the case of the women, relatively formal clothing. At the sales conference it makes a refreshing change to let people wear casual attire. Sales directors with a keen sense of observation will learn much from this exercise. Off-duty clothes are often a strong clue to a person's true personality.

That dour rep from your northern territory, for example, who is usually a pinnacle of sobriety in his charcoal-grey two-piece – you didn't expect to see him in a see-through blouse, Cuban heels and a beret, did you?

And as for Miss Giggleswick, the junior salesgirl on the team – did anybody realise she had such long bronzed legs? And was such a devastating expert in karate?

A certain amount of relaxed behaviour is inevitable at the sales conference, but sales management should make it abundantly clear beforehand that drunkenness and other anti-social capers are forbidden. An unnecessary and heavy-handed caveat perhaps? Not really.

Salespeople with monstrous hangovers are not receptive on the morning after, and the platform speakers don't want to address a roomful of flatulent zombies. Striking a balance, therefore, between rigid discipline and ragged free-wheeling is both crucial and delicate.

It sometimes helps to set a theme for the conference, a central idea around which the rest of the programme can be constructed.

If your company opts for play acting as a conference policy – and by that I mean simulating real sales situations with 'buyers' putting up objections and resistance – don't fall into the trap of over-exaggeration.

You will get the occasional wag who thinks it's highly

amusing to act out the difficult buyer like the living reincarnation of Attila the Hun. This will not be helpful.

If you detect that closing the sale is an area that needs attention, then try and honestly replicate real-life situations and seek practical solutions.

If you can find one, it might even pay to invite an actual customer along to the conference and let him face a sales pitch from one of your whizz kids. Be careful, though. If an aspiring sales-star upstages a client in front of an adoring audience of colleagues, he or she could well become an *ex*-client!

13
Delegation – the clean desk syndrome

To some sales managers, delegating responsibility to their subordinates is as painful as having a tooth hacked from the gum with a cold chisel. They are the ever-busy types who rack up sixteen hours a day and arrive home exhausted, full of complaints about the pressure they're under and how, without their own unrelenting efforts, the whole operation would flush down the tubes. I once worked for a manager like this who was so paranoid about keeping everything close to his chest, he used to get to the office before staff arrived and open their mail. Part of his reasoning was that if you didn't stay a jump ahead of your sales team, they would turn round and steal your job from under you. His pathological belief in the theory of conspiracy was so profound that it eventually became a self-fulfilling prophecy and he was removed from office by the board of directors after a staff meeting. Quite simply, he had so starved his subordinates of information and responsibility that they had become commercial eunuchs, dependent on his erratic whims for the smallest scrap of data. Fearful of his crumbling position, he would even deliberately organise a crisis – designed to break as soon as he went on holiday so that he could fly back and 'solve it', thus underlining his indispensability.

Although the poor fellow was an extreme case, he does have counterparts in many sections of British industry today – and they are very bad news indeed.

What sales managers must understand from their very first day in the job is that they will not be judged by *what they do themselves* or even by *how much* they do themselves. What their bosses will be looking for is how well they have managed the skills and resources of their department and how successful they have been in achieving the company's goals. A sophisticated board of directors will not be interested in a boastful catalogue of long hours worked or colourful tales of orders won *only* by the superhuman intervention of the irreplaceable manager. The art of sales management is in releasing the energies of your team and letting *them* sprint away in the pursuit of excellence. They will only be able to do this if they are given strong leadership, all the support services your budget will allow, and a measure of real responsibility that enhances their status not only in the eyes of their customers, but also in their own eyes. This last bit is not frothy rhetoric. Nothing crushes the spirit of a salesperson more than being told in front of a customer, for example, that the sales manager is standing by in the background to sort out any problem that may arise. What this particular approach implies is that the poor booby of a salesperson is going to screw-up anyway and Mr or Ms Big will be on hand to perform his or her tediously familiar Captain Wonderful act.

There is another side-effect which springs directly from the sales-manager-who-refuses-to-delegate syndrome, and it is potentially damaging for any marketing company that operates in a competitive arena. Put bluntly, it will be like an oak tree with rotten, wasted roots – all impressive foliage at the top and decay just below the surface. 'Strength and depth' are three words that every sales manager should pin on the wall. You should rejoice in seeing your staff grow in stature and ability. You should positively *want* them to be eager for advancement and you should even be prepared to say, 'I intend to train and encourage my deputy to be capable of taking over from me as soon as possible.'

Sales managers don't get fired for building a team of élite high-performers – indeed, it's about the best set of credentials you can ever show to your board – what sales managers do get fired for is *failure*. Failure to motivate the sales team, failure to *keep* them motivated, failure to achieve results. It's the bottom line that counts, not the grovelling time-sheet that shows the hours of sacrifice put in by a sales manager too selfish, too frightened or too incompetent to make the best of that scarce and precious resource – the salespeople.

Having waxed enthusiastic about the need to delegate, am I not erring on the side of lazy sales management where *everything* is shunted sideways and downwards while the manager slopes off with his cronies to play golf? Well, obviously not. Certain fundamental decisions and problems must always remain the strict responsibility of the sales manager. Here's a few of them.

1 Hiring people.
2 Firing people.
3 The selection of sales training programmes.
4 Budgetary control, including expenses.
5 Development of the fundamental sales story or 'pitch'.
6 Tackling customers who have become bad debts.
7 Planning and organising the sales conference.
8 Pricing. And getting the right price for the product or service.
9 Target-setting.
10 Negotiating commission scales or bonus deals within the company.
11 Recommending and *promoting* salary increases within the department.
12 Staff welfare. It's *you* they talk to if they have personal

problems, bad debts, pregnant girl friends, drunken boy friends, or visions of hell every time they wake up on Monday morning.

13 The creation of sales literature (style and content).
14 All internal negotiations with other departments (accounts, research, personnel, factory, transport, advertising, computers).
15 Profit. *You're* the manager. It's bottom-line time, baby.

I remember some years ago visiting the sales director of a major American life assurance company in New York. This man, still in his early thirties, was responsible for an operation that wrote in excess of three hundred million dollars worth of business every year. In spite of the awesome scale of his job and the grandeur of his office (to my impressionable eyes it seemed like an oak-panelled ballroom) his large Louis XIV desk was empty of all documents save one – a single sheet of paper on which had been typed a short checklist. I asked him about it and he explained that it was his '*get done this day*' list, a series of objectives, ranked in order of importance, that he had to accomplish.

During my half-hour with him, there were no frenetic phone calls, no aides rushing in with crisis messages; all was calm and peaceful, and yet he exuded considerable power and authority. Here was a man who clearly understood how to motivate a huge sales force spread across the whole of the United States.

'Listen,' he said to me when I asked him about his job, 'I put a lot of energy into selecting and training my sales people and then I make sure they get all the information and support they need to hack it in the ruthlessly competitive life market. It's rather like driving a Rolls-Royce – you *know* what's under the bonnet is the best in the world

– all you have to do is operate the pedals and steer it in the direction *you* want it to go.'

I've always believed that paperwork has been the death of many a sales manager or director, although a certain amount is, alas, unavoidable. I loathe long memos, which usually conceal a great deal more than they ever reveal, and I much prefer to speak directly with colleagues. Remember, no really good idea needs more than one side of an A4 sheet to state its basic case. Apart from which, it is a good discipline for salespeople to learn brevity in their written work. If somebody sends me a thirty-page position paper, I simply won't read it – unless it has a half-page summary attached. I take the same view of a salesperson's call reports. Unless *real* information is imparted, they can rapidly develop into a chore for both writer and recipient. A sharp sales manager won't tolerate guff and padding which a too bureaucratic approach can often produce. Insist on the *meat* and not the whole sandwich. It can help to draft out a formula that each salesperson follows when writing a report. At the end of the day there is no substitute for a face-to-face meeting between manager and rep. You can learn more in twenty minutes over a glass or two of champagne talking with your salespeople than struggling through brick-thick reports of balls-aching turgidity. So to stay sharp and streetwise and on top of your job, aim to have a clean desk and a *very* large wastepaper basket.

And trust your salesperson. They'll deliver if you delegate sensibly – and *their* success, remember, is yours too.

14
The sales party – paper hats and Dutch courage?

There are few spectacles more likely to plunge my spirits into a trough of despair than that of the traditional office party. Here, the grisly charade of English people enjoying themselves with grim determination is raised to a kind of naff art form. The brightly decorated accounts department hung with awful paper bells; the atmosphere a mixture of artificial mateyness and sexual longing, causing normally respectable and dull people to behave like extras in a remake of *The Last Days of Pompeii*. The reason for all this glutinous buffoonery is obvious, at least to me.

The office is not a palace of delights, and no amount of tinsel and men in funny hats will make it so. The party is also doomed to fail because people working in a variety of disciplines find it hard to behave naturally in such a contrived atmosphere. What *does* the ageing rep discuss with Miss Mablethorpe of engineering behind that battered filing cabinet? And does the financial director really enjoy talking about football with the office junior, who invariably ends up by being sick in his waste-paper basket? No, the only place for a staff party, as opposed to an office party, is somewhere as far away from the office as possible. Which brings me to a subtle variation of this annual celebration.

The sales department party. This should be an exclusive, deliberately élitist affair. Indeed, it is my recommendation that *all* departments should hold their own in addition to the big company bash. There is absolutely nothing wrong with each and every group having a celebration that is theirs and theirs alone – even if they have to pay for it out of their own pockets. Such an occasion consolidates feelings of team spirit and reinforces the concept that each discipline within a company or organisation is *special* – as indeed it is.

This has a particular importance to salespeople, who are the company's representatives to the world outside. A well-run, highly motivated sales department displays tribal characteristics which are more pronounced than you are likely to encounter among, say, time-and-motion study engineers. A shrewd sales manager will try to keep this fierce tribal flame alive, and one of the ways to do this is to organise a really memorable sales-team party *at least twice* a year.

Why not once? Well, once appears like a grudging concession and salespeople are a breed who half-believe in that frayed old maxim that nothing succeeds like excess. Under no circumstances invite wives, husbands, sweethearts, uncles or any other outsiders. They can go to the major company do – and a very good thing too. The sales party is, on the face of it, designed to let the whole sales team relax and enjoy themselves in an atmosphere of bonhomie and self-congratulation, but it also serves a much more fundamental purpose. It acts as an adhesive, binding the team together much like a mess party in a crack cavalry regiment where shared common experience and mutual goals are vital for survival. Unless you have experienced the electricity of a group of successful salespeople at play you will probably think I am being obsessively silly – even pedantic – about the value of a sales party.

I happen to believe that great sales teams find their

work and pleasure blurring into each other – and it is a condition to be encouraged.

It also enhances the value of a sales staff party if sales management plays a minimal role in organising it. Let the team pick the venue, decide the theme, select the menu, the music and all the rest of it. The sales manager should be there, of course – but as a *guest* of the team. Much can be learned by observing salespeople at play, even if you do get the occasional ear-bashing. Everybody, salespeople included, should ideally have positive feelings about the company they work for – after all, they do spend a lot of their waking lives *at work*. Good management includes striving to make the work process as enjoyable as possible. The sales party is just another brick in the wall, and one which the aspiring sales manager would be ill-advised to ignore.

15
Selling to our American cousins – communications customs and the culture shock

There exists a dangerous myth among salespeople that the rep whose job takes him abroad frequently has obtained a more glamorous niche than his colleagues who are, for example, confined to London, Manchester or Penge. Of course, if your taste runs to a fanatical love of airport departure lounges, oblique telephone systems and frequent bouts of Montezuma's revenge, then the overseas sales post is just the thing for you. Personally I enjoy foreign travel, but my good fortune has made it possible for my trips to be of a short duration – I don't think I would wax hysterically enthusiastic over a two-year posting to Borneo or even Moose Jaw, USA.

For the man or woman who needs brief but effective forays into the overseas markets there are pitfalls to be avoided and fundamental ground rules to be observed. Perhaps the most important and yet the most simple is to *prepare yourself well in advance.*

In an ideal world, the salesperson would be fluent in several languages but, alas, we British are notoriously chauvinistic about learning other people's tongues. There are honourable exceptions, of course. An old friend of mine sells British know-how to developing nations who need bridges or salt-water ports built in their arid and often uncomfortably hostile countries. Being a natural linguist – and remarkably conscientious into the bargain – he has established a reputation for reliability and trust that would be impossible for a Britisher trying to communicate in pidgin English or through a native translator.

If, like the majority of us, however, you aren't a whizz with languages and your French is strictly O level, the next most vital thing you must address yourself to is *preparation*. Not just of your product and its effectiveness, or even of its adaptability in different climates or geographical locations – but of how you will perceive the social and cultural environment of the country you plan to visit.

America may at first appear to be the most straightforward. We share a common language, don't we? Pretty well all salesmen and saleswomen have been exposed to American culture via television, cinema and popular literature and it's hard to believe there is a single person in the British Isles who hasn't met and talked with an American tourist or serviceman and his family.

The conclusion therefore is that we know what makes our American cousins tick. The reality when the British salesperson steps off the plane is quite different.

The American business scene, particularly in New York, is unlike anything you will encounter in a single European city. The culture is an exciting mix of ethnic variables but predominantly Jewish. The pace of the city is frenetic, and New York businesspeople waste no time on the more stylised forms of polite pre-business intercourse. The British salesperson must be prepared to be brief, concise and *very* convincing. Long preambles, which normally precede the set-piece sales presentation in Europe, are the kiss of death in New York.

But although speed and cogency are key factors, it's a mistake to assume that New Yorkers are all crude, impatient hustlers who speak with a Brooklyn drawl. They are shrewd, articulate, often remarkably well read and they are used to thinking on their feet. What is more, they actually *like* salespeople. This is in itself a refreshing change from the usual sniffy attitude still encountered in many parts of the United Kingdom. The British salesperson abroad, alas, still has a lingering reputation as a dilettante, and any hint of the laconic approach will only succeed in irritating the busy New York buyer.

On the plus side, an English accent, unless it's one of our more opaque regional variations, is a genuine asset. So – in New York, prepare your pitch with care, be punctual, be brisk, and be ready to make your proposition in about half the time you would normally take.

Another tip, New York businesspeople are, by and large, conservative. Dark suits, white shirts and sensible shoes – and their equivalent for women – are the order of the day. If you come swanning off Madison Avenue in a Prince of Wales check, chukka boots and a monocle, you may end up in the 2nd Precinct on a charge of impersonating an idiot. In short, *don't* try and palm yourself off as a stage Englishman – New Yorkers are too shrewd for that and they can spot a phoney a mile away.

In Los Angeles, however, the contrast in style and pace couldn't be more marked. To some it represents the ultimate laid-back society with perpetual sunshine, an abundance of wealth and an inexhaustible parade of bronzed and delicious Californian youngsters. Clothes are either sporty – tennis shoes, slacks or jeans; or outrageous – I once saw the chairman of a medium-sized corporation in a pink blazer and white shorts.

If your business takes you to the very best sections of Los Angeles – like Beverly Hills, Bel-Air, Brentwood or Malibu – you will, on first sight, be stunned by the cornucopia that presents itself to you. Hollywood – incidentally a rather vague, sprawling part of the city and now a great deal less fashionable than it used to be – was once described by that great American humourist S. J. Perelman as 'toytown for grown-ups'. Do not be deceived, however.

So You Want To Be A Sales Manager?

Los Angeles is a cruel and ruthlessly competitive place –
more of a sprawling suburb than a city, where the triple
gods are money, youth and hyperbole. Here, personal
appearance is so obsessively important to Californians that
it has become something of a religion. Virtually anything
goes – provided you have the courage to carry it off – but
you are less likely to succeed if you are overweight, wear
conservative clothes or smoke cigarettes. Cigarettes? Yes,
I'm afraid fags are about as popular as herpes – the Californians are on a huge no-smoking and better-health kick,
and there is no group of people on earth who embrace
new causes with such dedicated fanaticism. And if you're
a saleswoman, it does help to be well-groomed, well-
tanned, well-made-up, blonde and more than usually well-
endowed. Trivial? Certainly. Chauvinistic? Absolutely. But
that's how the cookie crumbles in the Golden State.

This said, however, the aspiring salesperson must be
polished, articulate and just as determined as their
counterparts in New York. The main difference is style.

Business deals with so many noughts attached that they
resemble telephone numbers are frequently conducted at
the poolside in surroundings that, superficially at least,
appear more suited to a vacation than a work environment.

Be prepared to meet – as I once did – the vice-president
of a major corporation wearing a Mickey Mouse hat in
the office. If you succeed in winning orders – whatever it
is you are selling – you will be a hero. Californians worship
success; failure, to them, is a contagious disease to be
shunned at all costs. And if you are a loser, you will be
made to feel like a box of dirty laundry. If failure happens
to *you* in California, there's only one thing you can do.
Pack your suitcase and quit town. An oversimplification?
Not really. The shallow, success-at-any-price culture of
Los Angeles can inflict vicious wounds on your already
dented ego if you hang around whining about your misfor-

tune. Even the barman in your hotel will turn sour if you unload tales of lost orders and missed opportunities on him over your early evening cocktail. What *he* wants to hear, as you sip your excruciatingly dry, inordinately large martini, is that you are a winner – a person who has vanquished all odds to come first in whatever race it was you were running.

Elsewhere in the United States Britishers are generally well received by their American hosts – and it is this fund of genuine goodwill which, personally, I have found most stimulating.

In Virginia and the Deep South you can be yourself – here the people are polite, thoughtful and responsive to the British approach. And you won't be expected to wear funny clothes. Society is formal, and behaviour patterns elegant and refreshingly old-fashioned.

Americans do like the British, and too often, alas, we respond by being either snooty or patronising – even in Las Vegas, surely the most dynamically hideous place on the face of the earth.

Fortunately I have not been called upon to conduct business in the desert resort. My only visit was, spuriously, for pleasure. In Vegas, I am convinced, whatever modest powers of persuasion I may possess would meet before a maelstrom of unashamed vulgarity.

In summary, be assured that a warm welcome awaits most British salespeople when they cross the Atlantic, provided that what is offered:

1 is relevant to the market
2 is of high quality
3 is keenly priced
4 can be delivered quickly
5 is unique

And, finally, provided that the salesperson lucky enough to be sent there is prepared to work harder, longer and against stiffer competition than they ever believed possible.

Good luck – and don't forget to chat with those helpful people at the American Embassy in Grosvenor Square before you go – they'll give you a refreshing taste of what to expect when you get to the other side.

16
Remuneration – how much should your salespeople earn and must there be a limit?

Next to expenses and company cars, commission earnings or sales bonuses give rise to more angst and internal company jealousy than any other single issue. One of the most difficult and yet crucial decisions a company has to make is how it plans to remunerate its sales force. The approach varies enormously, even in the United States, where stupendous commission earnings are commonplace. Some corporations favour straight salary, others straight commission. Yet a third group choose a carefully calculated mixture of the two. In this country, where more and more marketing companies are goal or achievement orientated, the debate ebbs and flows with advocates on both sides claiming that their method is far superior.

A great deal, of course, depends on the nature of the business in which you operate. If any single method appears to be emerging as most favoured, it is the salary-plus-commission – usually with clearly defined upper limits on the earnings package.

In certain markets, where cold-canvassing and pioneer work is the norm, commission-only can be an excellent incentive for the salesperson and a no-lose proposition for his company. If you don't deliver – runs the argument – neither do we. Conversely, if you strike gold, we'll let a little rub off on you too. In reality, it never works quite as simply as this and many a scheme hatched in the board-room and blessed by all present, financial director included, has given rise to anguish of a scale usually associated with the sack of Rome or an outbreak of bubonic plague.

During the very early days of ITV, there was a top salesman hired by an important company to head their advertising sales operation. It was a new industry and nobody really knew just how long it would take for the companies granted franchises to amortise their start-up expenses and break into profit. This particular man had agreed a deal with his company based on the mutual assumption that the level of sales would remain flat for at least two years while the new-fangled concept of television advertising took gradual root among potential customers. Sceptics even predicted that ITV would be no more than a flash in the pan and that serious growth was an illusion. Agreeing a commission scale in this quasi-pessimistic atmosphere meant that nobody paid much attention to its escalating nature, particularly as the really serious money could only be earned by the salesman when revenue exceeded levels far beyond even the most optimistic estimates.

In the event, ITV revenue took off, as predicted, somewhat sluggishly, and the salesman's earnings were small. Then after a couple of years, there was an explosion of growth and the revenue figures went rocketing off the graph. Suddenly the company had a salesman earning twice as much as the chairman. With gritted teeth and expressions of baffled fascination, the rest of the board watched the seemingly inexorable rise in the wealth of their sales chief. Soon he was driving his own Bentley and holidaying on a yacht in the South of France. His contract was scrutinised by lots of men with tiny, wrinkled foreheads in smoke-filled rooms but it was found to be watertight – and had a couple of years to run.

When renewal time did eventually arise, and a dramatically revised commission package was tabled by the company – generous by most standards, but nevertheless a fraction of the vast amounts earned in those halcyon early days – the sales chief, now hooked on a lifestyle that would have made a Maharajah look like a derelict, refused to sign the renewal. Result: very bad news for both the sales chief and the company. They lost a brilliant executive and he forfeited a glittering career. In my view, both were at fault as a result of those two demons that bedevil so many negotiations over salespeople's remuneration – jealousy on the one side and greed on the other. Whether you choose commission, basic salary or a combination of both, you will encounter these two demons if you fail to establish *first of all*, the company's financial objectives, its *minimum* profit levels and the *absolute* cost of any particular bonus or commission scheme.

Your financial director should be able to assist when you start putting your plans together. Let's assume, for the sake of illustration, that your company turns over five million pounds a year. Its projected annual profit before tax is, say, 10 per cent or £500,000.

What you need to thrash out with your financial director is how much *additional commission* your company can afford to pay out for every extra £100,000 of revenue (not profit), your salespeople produce. The amount will vary, of course, from company to company but it does help to have a clear view of these two figures before you set targets. In some industries, there are only limited increased costs associated with increased income – and commission, therefore, can be generous. Even in the highly competitive manufacturing industry, economies of scale *can* make more sales equal more profit – but not always.

Be careful. Listen to your accountant or financial director, *and only* present your proposals to the board or your immediate superiors if you are absolutely certain they have his or her support.

I favour bonus or commission schemes based upon *whole team* efforts rather than individual targets, but in certain businesses the one-man-one-target philosophy can work very effectively. It's not easy to keep *all* your sales-people motivated if one of them has a special arrangement on bonuses or commission and the others don't. It's also tough for a sales manager to carve up his sales territory or customer allocation in a way that gives each salesman an equal chance of high performance.

Whatever method you choose, it should be one that gives both the company and the sales team complete satis-faction. Any arrangement that is perceived to be lop-sided, or heavily weighted in favour of one or other party will eventually prove to be counter-productive, or in extreme cases, literally destructive.

But you must educate your board to rejoice in the high earnings of your sales team – provided they are based upon sturdy foundations. Well, should there be an upper limit on salespeople's earnings? The question is debated with vigour in most business communities all over the world. As I am biased, it will come as no surprise to hear that I favour the no limit whatsoever philosophy. Catch 22 is making absolutely certain you have the gearing right, and that in itself is a considerable management skill.

Given that your scheme meets all the company criteria associated with profit levels, dividend policy and all the other checks and balances necessary for board approval, then it matters not a jot if the salespeople as individuals become as rich as Croesus.

Finally, when you are scratching your head over what sort of incentive package will suit your own particular sales team, here are a few things to remember that might help.

If you favour a *commission only* scheme (which I don't

recommend unless you have only part-timers or freelancers on your staff), then be certain to spell out the downside risks of such an arrangment – i.e. zero income. In my experience, commission only can produce a sense of greed or desperation in a salesperson who is running through a bad patch. The temptation exists to force a sale at all costs, using dubious, high-pressure tactics, and you shouldn't want desperate men representing you – ambitious and eager certainly, but not desperate.

If it's established company policy to remunerate sales staff by salary alone – and in many organisations this is the only sensible method – then you will still have to find ways of providing incentives to greater effort. A sales team that only delivers average performance and draws average salaries is no good to man nor beast.

Perhaps you should consider results-linked prizes (holidays abroad, video cameras, suit vouchers, etc) as the much needed spur. If your company frowns on such fripperies, then you have got to be a very determined and persuasive sales manager indeed when it comes to the time for annual salary reviews. The carrot, in whatever form, is infinitely more effective than the stick if you want to see your salespeople operate in the fast lane – and what sales manager doesn't?

If you decide that a combination of salary and commission is the route for your company, then make the basic salary respectable – even generous. Bonus or commission earnings can be as dramatic as you think fit – provided you remember the old axiom: 'Only *exceptional* performance deserves *exceptional* rewards.' And when your star rep earns more than the production director or chief financial officer, smile – you've probably picked a winner.

17
The right moment to make a pitch – a cautionary tale

It is nine-thirty on a warm June evening and the fabled Orient Express is snaking its way through sleepy vineyard country, towards the Swiss border en route for Venice.

In the piano bar the wall lamps are glowing softly behind silk shades and the buzz of conversation is punctuated by the discreet popping of champagne corks and the tinkle of ice in Waterford crystal.

Men and women cluster around the pianist as he runs his fingers lazily over the ivories, producing with apparently no serious effort a marvellous and lilting version of Cole Porter's 'Night and Day'.

The men are wearing dinner jackets and black ties, the women long silky dresses, their hair shining, their diamonds sending out sharp, lancing reflections as they move their hands to light cigarettes.

From the open door which leads beyond this elegant salon drifts the merest hint of rich food. Tantalisingly it mingles with the exotic perfumes and cigar smoke around the bar.

A young waiter glides between the crowded sofas, balancing a silver tray laden with champagne. Past the gleaming reflections on satiny wood panelling and through the big picture windows darkening countryside flashes by. We see the stripe of a distant river, copper-coloured in the pale moonlight, and a huge forest crouching like a massed army on the curved hillside.

I observe this most pleasing scenario from my corner seat by the piano. The Dom Pérignon '72 is ice-cold and I am pondering on whether to start dinner with chilled soup or smoked salmon and caviare.

At this precise moment an outlandish figure appears in the doorway from the sleeping compartments. He wears bright pink golfing slacks, white shoes and a flimsy cotton shirt, unbuttoned to the navel, exposing a hairy paunch. A gold chain thicker than a child's finger dangles from his throat. His hair, although white, is elaborately waved and arranged carefully, but unsuccessfully, to conceal a bald pate. He is obviously an American.

Impervious to the ridiculous sight he presents among all these elegant people, he goes to the bar and orders something unpleasant with cherries in it.

The barman, trained to within an inch of his life, winces discreetly, but serves the confection as if he is handling a live grenade.

The man in pink trousers downs the drink with a single gulp and lights a pale green cigar which looks, without a soupçon of exaggeration, just like a smouldering cucumber. He then moves towards a group of people with their backs to him and I hear him vainly try to insinuate himself into their company. 'Hi. I'm Al. Hell of a train isn't it?'

The group nods politely, but by a subtle display of body language indicates that he is unwelcome in their presence.

He shuffles to another group, who briefly succumb to his empty charm but then their eyes glaze over, and he tries his luck on a tall blonde with earrings the size of ducks' eggs. She is momentarily trapped, but rescue comes in the form of an Iranian businessman who leads the woman away.

Al is undaunted. He circulates on the outer fringe of

the salon like a persistent wasp. I strain to catch what he is saying, but only snatches are audible.

He produces a wallet from which visiting cards appear as if by magic. A dreadful realisation begins to steal over me. This awful man is a salesman. He is actually trying to pitch the people in the bar – oblivious to the fact that they regard him as an intrusive buffoon – with all the subtlety of an inflamed wart.

It occurs to me with dawning horror that it is only a matter of time before he gets round to my corner of the bar and turns his attentions to me. If I let slip that I too am a member of the selling trade all will be doomed.

I visualise the explosion of delight that will wreathe his bland features. A bangled, Neanderthal arm will encircle my shoulders as he recognises a fellow huckster! Drinks will be purchased – frothy creations with improbable names like 'Cowpuncher's Tonic' or 'Cleveland Chainsaw'.

He will cling limpet-like to my wife and me at dinner, winking and grimacing with a grotesque intimacy that chills the soul. Information about his family will be offered in Byzantine detail.

We will hear of his split-level, ranch-style pagoda in Philadelphia. His voice will drop an octave or two as he provides us with a blow-by-blow account of his recent vasectomy, his tendency to mild haemorrhoids, his plucky battle with gum-rot, the fraught web of his personal relationships, his meaningful dialogue with his analyst – inevitably a Hungarian emigré with a leatherette couch. We will learn of his struggle with 'sexual-identity-problems-at-this-moment-in-time'.

By the time coffee is served we will be soul mates. He will have extracted information from me like a dentist hacking out a dead molar with a cold chisel. Desperately, in self-defence I will deflect the conversation away from my own family history and he will spring into the void with devout enthusiasm.

As razor-thin chocolate mints are consumed and more coffee poured, he will sketch in his views of premature ejaculation, socialised medicine, the Reagan administration, cocaine-sniffing in California and the British Royal Family.

Eventually he will proffer his business card revealing his true colours as either an insurance salesman or a vendor of real estate in the Florida swamplands.

A naked panic engulfs me, but mercifully I am spared. His attention has been lassooed by a vast Canadian widow in a tent-like evening dress studded with rhinestones. He homes in like an Exocet missile and they lock together in a conversation of immediate and deep sincerity.

Later, in my elegant couchette, I lie awake as the train rackets through unseen tunnels and past sleeping farmland, pondering on the foolishness of the dreadful Al. Cold-canvassing on the Orient Express is not to my taste exactly, but if it has to be done at all it seems vital that the salesperson blends into the surroundings.

I doubt if Al made a single sale of whatever it was he was hawking, although I concede I could be wrong. To aspiring sales-stars I would only offer this advice: unless you have the hide of a rhinoceros and the discretion of a wounded buffalo you should try and anticipate the style and the surroundings of your intended prospects. To sell successfully is to gain people's confidence, and this is not achieved by jarring their sensibilities with a sledge-hammer.

There is a sequel to the story. Many months later I met a real-estate salesman in a Soho restaurant and we got chatting about how to identify new opportunities and avoid selling to 'brick-wall clients' who are hostile to commercial persuasion. Unprompted, he revealed that he travelled regularly on the Orient Express from London to Venice and found it a rich hunting ground for his high-priced real-estate propositions. Unlike the unfortunate Al, my friend becomes part of the stylish crowd on the train, always taking his wife and only hinting in the most gentle fashion imaginable that he sells land in Swiss ski resorts and vineyards in Tuscany. He understands the secret of good salesmanship; the customer has to believe *he* or *she* is making the decision to buy, and the salesperson is merely there to provide information.

In reality, of course, this particular real-estate man was exerting immense pressure on his potential clients, but it was subtle, restrained, brilliantly conceived and patiently executed.

I'll wager that pink-trousered Al wouldn't have recognised him as a fellow salesman in a thousand years.

So, research the environment in which you plan to sell and try to adjust your pace and your message to suit your surroundings.

In some situations the 'belt-it-to-them-between-the-eyes' routine actually works. Selling sheep in an Australian market, for example. Subtle nuances of style would be lost in such a maelstrom of sweaty turbulence. Only a nose-picking, beer-swilling, all-belching, all-scratching swaggerer is going to catch anybody's attention.

Likewise the activities on the floor of one of the City of London's money markets, where well-dressed men with carnations in their buttonholes scream and bellow like maddened bull elephants. To fail to judge the environment in which you may sell can lead to frustration and repeated failure.

On my first visit to Japan I had listened carefully to wise counsels about the intricate nature of the Tokyo business scene. I knew that the smash-and-grab approach would be a disaster and that I had to observe the rituals so beloved of my important hosts. Written appointments had been made and I had prepared brief presentations to give to each client I called on.

One morning at the Regency Hyatt Hotel, as I sipped coffee overlooking the city's Manhattan-like skyline, the phone rang. It was the secretary of a client I was due to see later that day. She confirmed the time of the meeting – 11.30 a.m.– and then asked me how long *exactly* my presentation would take.

Twenty-eight minutes, I told her, having rehearsed it to the second over the previous weeks at home. After breakfast I caught a cab to the Ginza, Tokyo's business and shopping area – a vast web of boulevards, fabulous department stores and narrow side-streets crammed with boutiques, restaurants, showrooms and curio shops.

My client was located in a skyscraper of awesome proportions. The lobby was a symphony of grained marble and soaring glass panels. Fountains of pink water bubbled in a huge circular mosaic and from the central cupola depended a modern chandelier like a vast melting toffee of bronze fibreglass.

I caught the elevator and was rocketed twenty-five floors to an elegant suite of offices and greeted by a pretty Japanese girl in Christian Dior clothes. She showed me into a circular boardroom, panelled in dark oak and dominated by an enormous table surrounded by thirty chairs.

At the top end of this gleaming slice of African teak sat a half-circle of six sombre Japanese men in identical grey suits. They rose as I entered and we went through the bowing and smiling routine.

Introductions over, I opened my flip charts and placed them on the table. At previous presentations I had used slides and tapes, but today was rather more basic. I launched into my act, speaking carefully lest my enthusiasm blur the compelling nature of my pitch, and I was received with rapt but polite attention.

I was through in twenty-seven minutes, just ahead of schedule, and was about to invite questions when the boardroom door opened and the Japanese girl appeared carrying a tiny gong. This she struck with an even tinier padded hammer. The effect was instantaneous. The six Japanese rose to their feet, smiling, hands were extended for me to shake and I was shown out of the room.

At first I was perturbed. The smooth finality of the proceedings seemed odd, and I wondered whether I had committed some ghastly social blunder.

I certainly hadn't mentioned Pearl Harbour or the Burma Railway – as far as I could recall. The mystery was soon cleared up when the youngest of the six men reappeared, still smiling, and offered me tea.

His board colleagues, he explained, were at an all-day annual meeting, but had broken off for half an hour specifically because I had asked to give them a presentation. It was a privilege to have them interrupt their important deliberations to hear my little speech, and I told him so.

The incident with the gong was even more interesting. If I had been overrunning my thirty minutes, interrupting me verbally would have been discourteous, but by sending in the secretary with gong and hammer any rudeness was prevented and we all responded like boxers breaking at the sound of the bell.

I learned much more about the nuances and rhythms of Japanese business while I was there, and the system fascinated me. Nearly all my contacts have proved to be 'slow burners', by which I mean nobody makes snap decisions. You have to win their confidence over a long time before you can clinch any serious deals.

Every sales situation is different and we can learn a lot

from watching the complicated rituals that take place in foreign countries.

I'm told that in parts of Borneo it is a sign of goodwill to be offered the chieftain's wife for the night. It's amazing what salespeople will put up with just to get an order.

18
The salesperson's bedside companion

In the last chapter I described how I witnessed misplaced sales enthusiasm on the Orient Express when a pitchman vainly tried to interest wealthy customers in his proposition and received instead hostility and indifference. His mistake was not that his product or service was wrong but that he had *misread the environment* in which his prospects were placed. They were, by and large, wealthy and in the jargon of the researchers 'a prime target market' for real estate or some other expensive item or service. What their mood indicated, however, if the salesman had bothered to read it properly, was *that they were not in the buying mode at that moment.* The environment was wrong – but only because the salesman had failed to melt into it and become a part of the ambience his prospects were wallowing in.

It must be clear, therefore, that reading the mood of your customers and appreciating the environment in which they are situated are essential if a salesperson stands even the slightest chance of success. There is only one thing worse than misreading the mood of your customers – and that is being in the right place at the right time with the prospects in a relaxed and receptive frame of mind *but having the totally wrong product to offer them.*

To illustrate what I mean let me take you back to the middle seventies when I made my first – and probably my only – trip across the Atlantic on the famous QE2.

Unlike the Orient Express, which is all too brief an

experience, five days at sea cocooned in luxury, fed, watered and wined like a Renaissance prince, actually alters the state of your mind. People who are by nature ambitious and driven, find, usually by the third day, that their appetite for relentless hard work is tempered by a delicious, creeping lethargy. The scramble to use the ship's telex or telephone begins to wane. Breakfast is taken later each morning. The post-lunch siesta stretches till four o'clock. And there is a sudden interest in reading the vintage wine list at least an hour before the evening meal.

On arrival in New York, however, when the stunning skyline of Manhattan looms on the horizon and the great ship bustles with activity, the thoroughly unwound executive starts coiling up again like the spring in a clockwork toy. By the time the ship is alongside the quay, jawlines are clenched and briefcases are being brandished like medieval battle banners as their owners prepare to meet the terrors of the New York business jungle.

The QE2, it has to be said, is not a replica of the old *Queen Mary* or any of those stunningly majestic liners that used to cross the Atlantic in the golden days between 1910 and the 1930s. She is a thoroughly modern ship, more like a hotel in Benidorm than the Ritz in Paris, with precious little veined marble, no Corinthian columns, hardly any dark wood panelling and no antique fireplaces or furniture. Service is brisk rather than elegant and although people do occasionally dress for dinner in first class, the feeling of grandness and – dare I say it – pomp is lacking.

One thing hasn't changed, though, and that is the average age of the ship's passengers. I was in my early forties at the time I sailed and I felt like a callow youth on his first outing. Snowy white heads, elastic ankle bandages, walking sticks, hearing aids and faint wheezing sounds provided the backdrop to what was, nevertheless, a most enjoyable experience.

The age syndrome was most marked during late evening when the largely geriatric clientele sloped off to bed at ten-thirty, leaving the band scraping away at their instruments to a near-deserted ballroom. It is true that I did encounter a seventy-year-old in the gymnasium one day, but he was an exception – an ex-boxer who still kept himself in shape by daily exercise. In such an environment, I remember thinking, certain sales propositions would go down like a lead balloon – string bikinis, twenty-year endowment policies, mortgages, racing bicycles, football boots and downhill skis. Others, however, would have found immediate favour with our elderly and largely charming fellow passengers.

A purveyor of goods and services designed specifically to appeal to the over-sixties could have a bonanza on the QE2. For all I know, even as I write these words, a clutch of enterprising salespeople are adjusting their black ties or shoulder straps before dinner and preparing to walk along those huge ship's corridors into a roomful of captive customers who will fall over themselves to purchase products or even ideas that will reflect and enhance their own particular needs.

So, if any of you smart-as-paint roller-skate salespeople or see-through T-shirt hucksters are planning a five-day blitz on a transatlantic liner – think again.

If, on the other hand, you specialise in 'no penalty' insurance for the over-fifties, retirement homes or fine jewellery – then happy hunting. But take it steady. Old doesn't mean gullible. Years of life's experiences make older people pretty shrewd – and they *will* listen to you if you remember that one day pretty soon you'll be old too.

Old salespeople do exist. Success is not the exclusive preserve of the sound of wind and limb. In New York in the 1980s, a seventy-six year-old insurance salesman was reported to be earning in excess of half a million dollars a year. Some of the most successful salesmen and saleswomen I have met don't even *look* like salespeople. OK – what are salespeople *supposed* to look like, I hear you ask.

Well, most of us have an Identikit picture of a smartly dressed man or woman who is pleasant, persuasive, articulate and energetic. Generally speaking, most successful people fall into this category. There exists, however, a minority who do not conform to this pattern at all. They are the mavericks, and they are a rare and special breed.

The cleverest among them, certainly that I have ever met, was a Canadian living in London whom I shall call Bob.

Bob was overweight, untidy, short of breath and socially inept. When I was first introduced to him I couldn't believe that anybody would hire him at all. But there he was, the advertising sales director of a specialist publication in a highly competitive market, and he looked as if he had just escaped from a refugee camp. Buttons were missing from his shirt and his suede shoes were scuffed and shiny.

His private life was a mess. His wife had left him, not surprisingly, and he lived in a small flat above a chemist's shop in a seedy part of London. Even his company car looked dusty, inside and out. My curiosity got the better of me, and while it would be an exaggeration to say I befriended him, I did have a drink with him on a half-dozen occasions to see if I could find out not only what made him tick, but how the hell he actually survived in the cut-throat world of space sales. Bob the maverick, I discovered, was one of the shrewdest operators in the game. How did he do it? Well, he possessed one extraordinary quality which, he admitted, he had discovered many years before. He was able to rouse people's sympathies. Not just a few people's sympathies, but everybody's.

In spite of his puffy body and shambolic appearance, he did resemble a sort of battered teddy bear and – perhaps most important of all – he was no threat to anybody. Men felt superior, even avuncular, when pearl-shaped Bob shuffled into their office. Women felt instinctively sorry for a man, deserted by his wife, who was so obviously in need of love, care and attention. And Bob *knew* it. He grinned sheepishly. He pulled the lobe of his ear, he adjusted his thick-lensed glasses and he mumbled his way through his sales pitch in a tone of voice that – on the face of it – invited instant rejection.

What happened? What happened is that Bob got business. Lots of it. Unbelievable? No. Absolutely true. Buyers used to joke about Bob phoning them at press deadlines and begging them, in halting tones, to take a space in his magazine. He'd mutter something about getting the chop if he didn't make targets, and although the ploy certainly didn't work every time, it worked *enough* times to become a permanent part of his insidious and cunningly worked out battle-plan.

He didn't mind being the butt of other people's jokes because, by accepting this role of submissive jester, he obtained and stored up an even greater supply of sympathy. And sympathy was Bob's most valued acquisition.

We drifted apart, but I heard that he continued to flourish like a dank weed in a garden of spectacular flowers, eventually moving from his apartment over the chemist's shop into a comfortable four-bedroomed house in Buckinghamshire.

The very last report, almost certainly apocryphal, was that his pathos and despair had melted the heart of a vulpine widow with considerable investments in Bolivian tin mines, who had married him and swept him off to her villa in Portugal, where, legend insisted, he spent his days drinking Krug champagne, smoking Havana cigars and gorging himself on Beluga caviare, smoked salmon and Viennese chocolate éclairs. I am half-inclined to believe the tale, fantastic though it is.

A word of warning. Bob was a rare creature, a man who was resilient enough to accept the world's cruel contempt and turn it skilfully to his own advantage. Unless you are convinced that you are one of nature's slobs and possessed of all the negative virtues with which Bob was so richly endowed, you would be advised to steer well clear of this route and concentrate on enhancing the more positive aspects of your personality.

19
High style or low flash – and does it matter?

Do you sincerely believe you've got high style? Or do you simply possess low flash?

At certain levels of your career a bit of low flash can actually be valuable – particularly among people who wouldn't recognise high style if it crawled up their trouser leg and chewed off their kneecap.

Some are luckier than others.

They acquire high style effortlessly, its prime requisite being that it is *always understated.* They don't necessarily have to spring from the loins of ducal families – indeed a few dukes' sons I could mention have achieved a level of oafishness undreamt of even among soccer hooligans. High style is as much an attitude of mind as anything else, and those who acquire it shine forth, as William Shakespeare said, like good deeds in a naughty world.

However, a word of caution.

A number – indeed a very large number of salespeople who have got to the top of their particular heap – will never possess high style. They will remain, their pink Rolls-Royces and gold wristwatches notwithstanding, practitioners of low flash. No amount of vintage port or Mediterranean sunshine will ever eradicate the fact that they are badly disguised yobboes at heart.

It is relatively easy for me to sketch a portrait of such a man. You will recognise him immediately. (Saleswomen can translate – I don't feel qualified to draw the female equivalent.)

He will be stocky, even thickset. His hands, in spite of the forty-quid manicure, will be those of a manual worker with individual fingers like pork sausages. His neck will wrinkle in early middle age, and around it he will place a variety of heavy gold chains. He will adopt an elaborately coiffed faintly 1950s hairstyle with tinting and rakish side-whiskers. He will favour safari suits in beige or pale blue and he will wear at least three chunky rings, a gold wrist-watch and a gold identity bracelet which weighs as much as your shoe.

His shoes will be of the built-up variety, giving him those extra inches he craves.

He will be a good chap basically, full of badinage and jokey reminiscence. He will drive a 'Roller' or a Jaguar and live in a big undistinguished house in North London or Essex – probably near Chingford, which he believes is 'real country'. He will drink rather a lot, preferring hard liquor poured into fat, cut-glass tumblers. He will be persuasive – naturally, he's a top salesman, remember – and he will possess an abundance of earthy charm.

He will have ironed out *most* of those rough vowel sounds – but the roughness will still rise to the surface, particularly when he's angry. Or drunk. He will never understand vintage wines, the decaying charm of Venice or the piercing pleasures of really tender, sophisticated sex. Being a brusque, 'leg-over' type of chap he will view such diversions as 'poncey'.

In expensive restaurants he will bully waiters and send food back, glaring and patting his wallet. His wife, Doreen, with a beehive hairdo and eighteen grand's worth of real diamonds round her turtle's throat, will still look like a barmaid from the Gorbals. Their children will invariably be called Sharon and Clint. Even now, with half a million in the bank, the family will still take a big suite at a Benidorm hotel for their annual holiday.

OK. Have you got the picture? That's *low flash*.

Bearing in mind that so many top salespeople will end up like the fellow I have just described, what, pray – you will be asking – is the point of acquiring high style?

Certainly, it is no guarantee of material success. Certainly it is a quality that will hardly be recognised by nine-tenths of the world's population – if *that*.

Why bother about it then?

Read on, you aspiring sales-star, and the truth, beautiful in all its manifestations, will be revealed to you in a trice or so. The possession of high style sets people apart from their fellows, and one of its greatest assets is that *no amount of money* can ever purchase it.

Elitist claptrap, do I hear you whine?

Not a bit of it, my friend. The mistake many ordinary salespeople make is to assume that high style is the exclusive preserve of the high born, that the smooth, omnipotent qualities which are its hallmark only reveal the inevitable fruits of a public school or Oxbridge education.

This is not so.

It helps, of course, if your interests extend beyond watching football and greyhound racing and if your palate revolts at the taste of English beer. You are also unlikely to be a candidate for high style if you were tattooed during your impecunious youth.

What then, would my Identikit high stylist be like?

Let it be said at once that he would need to be at least moderately successful – or poised on the brink of a glittering future. He will not be fat. Muscular leaness is ideal, although not of the half-starved whippet variety.

Medium to tall in height, he will reject the fancy, artificial hairstyles so popular among the low flash, and these days his hair will be shortish. It will not, however, look as if he has just had it cut – even when he *has* just had it cut.

He will wear English suits, Italian shoes and, just occasionally, American shirts.

Personal jewellery, or 'body furniture' will be kept to a minimum. He will never wear an identity bracelet.

He will have developed a keen sense of colour and design, and in spite of mild accusations about foppishness, will take as much interest in choosing the curtains as the woman in his life does. He will possess that elusive quality of apartness, even though he is by nature a people person.

Elegant, clean, well-groomed and athletic (high style is only possible if you are in good physical nick), he will be confident in the company of either clerks or princes. *This ability to mix effortlessly is perhaps the most critical aspect of the high style personality.* Salespeople, even those with an abundance of high style, will need to glide through life at all levels. Customers are customers, remember, even though they come on like rasping hooligans.

So the salesman with high style will not parade a ludicrous Bertie Wooster accent or a curly-brimmed bowler from St James. They would mark him as a toff, which he most certainly is not.

He will prefer L'Hôtel in Paris to any number of Holiday Inns, and even when he has made his first million he will never, under any circumstances, drive a Rolls-Royce with a gold mascot on the bonnet or one of those gross all-white bastardised Mercedes with TV aerials on the roof, much favoured by oily sheiks and bank robbers from Deptford. He will age gracefully with just a hint of silver at the temples.

He will not display his origins, whether they be a gypsy caravan in Tintagel or a stately home in Dorset. He will be twentieth-century man, polished, urbane, well-read, sexually alert.

Pardon?

Sexually alert does not mean coarsely randy like the low flash merchant. Whereas our tattooed, gold-chain strewn, blow-waved yobbo will look forward, with lip-smacking impatience, to a good screw, high style man will savour the anticipation of an evening's erotic frolicking with the same cool panache as if he were waiting for the curtain to rise at the Royal Opera House, Covent Garden.

High style man likes women, and is an accomplished performer in bed. He is a sensualist, rather than a stud. Low flash man knows what goes where and believes the quicker it all takes place the better.

The true importance of high style, however, isn't in the field of sexual prowess, or fashion, or in the knowledge of fine restaurants. It is important because it enables an ambitious salesperson to cross and re-cross social barriers and exploit all opportunities like a brilliant chess player.

Mr Low flash, swigging champagne by the side of his kidney shaped pool in Majorca, hi-fi blaring out 'The Best of Mantovani' or Matt Monro at the Copacabana, Luton, can never be certain people aren't laughing behind his back. Rich yobboes are always uneasy. The dropped aitch, the indiscreet belch, the sluttish wife and other social gaffes are ever lurking on the sidelines.

For high style man, driving his woman insane between black satin sheets for at least half an hour before final consummation, no such doubts exist. He is ready to make his sales pitch to king or costermonger – and feel perfectly at home with both.

Have a glance at these next few comparisons – they sum up the major point to watch for.

(A) *Dress appearance*

High style	Low flash
English suits in grey, fawn or dark blue	Hong Kong suits in pale blue
Gucci or Bally shoes – plain black or brown	All-white shoes. Most two-tone shoes
Cotton or silk shirts	Drip-dry nylon Short sleeves (ugh)
Black socks, always	Any coloured socks
Dark overcoats	Heavy trench coats with meaningless epaulettes
White raincoats	Black raincoats with little chains at the back
Silk knitted ties	Golf club or Royal Engineers type ties
Well-cut blazers	Blazers with badges on the breast pocket
Fob watches	Watch chains stretched across the waistcoat – very working class
Well-cut cords	Flared jeans
Canvas sailing trousers	The bottom half of a track suit
Brogues	All trainers or tennis shoes unless made by Gucci at vast expense
Brief, crutch-hugging underpants	Y-fronts in cream wool
Foulard scarves	Hats
Plain leather gloves in winter	All driving gloves with holes in the back
Small square Cartier watches or Rolex Oysters	Any watch with lots of knobs on and the time of day in sixteen countries

111

(B) *Motor vehicles*

Mini	Jaguar
Mercedes (except diesel)	Porsche
Ferrari	Rolls Royce
Bentley (if in plain colour)	Lotus
Daimler	Anything American except a 1956 Ford Thunderbird
Renault 5	Metro
Aston Martin Lagonda	Almost anything Japanese
Morris 1000 Traveller	Volvo Estate
An old Ford	A new Ford
An early Bugatti	An early Austin Princess
A yellow Suzuki Jeep	An orange van

(C) *Sexual locations*

On the floor of her flat	In the back of your car
Standing up in a hammock	Standing up in a football crowd (unless the match is in Buenos Aires)
On Concorde to New York	On the shuttle to Manchester
In the bath – preferably circular	In the kitchen
On the boardroom table	On the post room table
Before dinner at San Lorenzo	After a huge nosh at the Aberdeen Steak House
On the lawns at Glyndebourne during a performance of *Aida*	Behind the car park of the Stoat and Whistle during a darts match.

(D) *The home*

A flat in Chelsea	A maisonette in Putney
A Georgian manor house in Surrey	A Georgian-*style* mansion in Essex
Gravel drives	Tarmac drives
Silk lampshades	Chandeliers
Two matching sofas, in pastel or soft floral prints	White leather sofas with wrap-around end bits
No cocktail cabinet	A vast, musical cocktail cabinet
Plain curtains, swagged	Tassels on the end of pelmets
Plain carpets	Carpets which look like refugees from the Regal cinema with crowns and roses
Well-read books, including paperbacks. Lots of them on shelves.	Sets of 'improving' books with new stiff leatherette spines behind glass-fronted bookcases.
Black satin bedspreads	Pyjama cases in the shape of toy leopards with zips
A champagne bucket in the bathroom	A milk-shake dispenser in the bathroom

(E) *In the garden*

Statues (limited)	Gnomes
Sundials	Thatched bird houses
Live pheasants	Two Alsatians who defecate ceaselessly. One of them will be called Prince
Lawns	Rockeries
Gazebos	Sheds
Gardeners called Simon	Handymen called Alf

113

OK. Do you recognise yourself? And are you happy with what you see? Be honest. You may be able to kid yourself, but other people are not so gullible.

20
Indispensability, baiting the hook and other lessons

The difference between making yourself indispensable and just a plain nuisance is wafer thin.

Salesmen who need customers must themselves create and establish needs among those to whom they sell. And then satisfy those needs.

At its most crude and sinister, the drug-pusher provides an extreme example of this technique, but his vile trade depends on artificial means and has little to do with legitimate persuasion.

One of the surest ways for a salesperson to become indispensable is to anticipate the client's needs. No, this is not hocus-pocus. Let me give you an example, crude in its simplicity, natural in its application and highly effective in its execution.

I arrived late one evening in the city of Bangkok, tired after a boring flight from Japan. As we disembarked at Bangkok airport the heat smote us like an invisible wall. It was dark, and from beyond the tarmac perimeter I could see a tantalising glitter of lights that promised an exotic twenty-four hours in the ancient Siamese capital.

In truth, modern Bangkok is a sad place, its streets choked with battered, honking cars, its buildings crumbling, its economy heavily dependent on dubious sexual offerings, massage parlours and tourists.

My wife and I were only staying for one night, and on the recommendation of friends had booked into the

Oriental Hotel, which is situated like a colonial jewel on the banks of a seething river.

Struggling through Customs with suitcases and boxes of Havana cigars I was struck by the serene faces of the Thailanders, as they now prefer to be known.

As I squinted at incomprehensible signs and garish posters, a young man sprang in front of me and grinned amiably. 'You want a taxi,' he asked, seizing my wife's suitcase. We followed meekly and he led us through a jostling throng out into an inky black courtyard stuffed with cars and trucks and what appeared to be motorised rickshaws.

We climbed into a sedan which already had a driver at the wheel and its engine running. When I asked for the Oriental Hotel our guide, who had slid in beside the driver, turned and addressed us over the seat.

'My name is Van,' he said, 'I speak some English.'

In fact, his English was excellent and virtually self-taught. He couldn't have been much more than eighteen or twenty and he had never been to America or England in his life. The driver was his brother and they worked as a team.

Although I was tired, I was fascinated by the constant stream of patter he kept up. It was not the usual tourist crap which most guides learn like parrots, but an intelligent commentary on the city through which we now drove. What we could see at night was not very uplifting. Shuttered shops, neon-lit clubs, cracked pavements and collapsing slogan-daubed walls.

'Only one night in Bangkok?' said Van incredulously when I told him our travel plans.

'Yes,' I replied, 'but we want to see as much as possible.'

Van nodded eagerly. 'I fix tour,' he said. 'I can arrange a boat tomorrow early. We do river tour, holy temples, floating market, buy silk – good prices no rip-off.'

'How much?' I asked.

It was then that Van revealed his true skills as an instinctive saleman.

'Fifty dollars the whole package. You pay me, I do the deals, arrange boat, temple guides, visit to crocodile farm, amazing snake-wrestling, curio shops, back in the hotel by one o'clock.'

'All this in a morning?' I asked.

Van nodded. 'We start at eight. I be at your hotel in the lobby at five minutes before. You get a discount you pay me half now.'

I was so impressed with his enthusiasm that I gave him twenty-five dollars there and then, and we shook hands in the taxi.

Here was a salesman incarnate. He had wit, charm, loquacity, persistence and, above all, the natural ability to make himself an indispensable prop.

Certainly I could have rejected his blandishments and looked for another guide in the morning, but his approach was hard to resist. And he delivered.

At eight sharp next day we were aboard a creaking motorised barge with Van, a lugubrious skipper and his exquisite three-year-old daughter.

The tour was amazing. Van had contacts everywhere – he even knew the peasants in the extraordinary floating market, a narrow strip of river surrounded by jungle where old Thai women sold you fruit and flowers from their frail canoes.

We saw the crocodile farm and some pretty sleazy snake-charming – if a half-asleep cobra being dragged by its tail out of a sack can be described as snake-charming!

And we walked up several hundred steps at a stunning temple with crenellations like something out of a mad theatrical designer's rejected sketch book. And, yes, we bought silk. About eight miles of it, as I recall. A closed

117

shop was opened for us after Van spoke a few words through a barred window to the owner.

Finally, we were back at the Oriental Hotel in time for a late lunch prior to dashing to the airport again, care of Van's brother, to catch our Karachi-London plane.

Now that was salesmanship.

Once in Soho's Berwick Street Market there used to be a wonderful character who styled himself 'Tosher the Tie King'. He was a consummate salesman who ran through a superb sequence of attracting your attention, whetting your appetite, making you laugh, creating instant demand, naming a price, closing the sale and collecting your money. It was perfect, text-book technique that scored every time. Tosher had razor-sharp wit and an awesome line in salty repartee. I can honestly say that I never saw him at a loss for words and he was at his scintillating best when he was faced with an initially indifferent crowd.

Drab clerks munching their lunchtime sandwiches would stop and look bleakly at the little whippet of a man with his jaunty Trilby and garish handpainted tie. Tosher would fix them with a basilisk stare and employ his mock-insulting routine.

'Look at that geezer's tie!' he would say. 'I've seen better bits of string holding up a tramp's trousers. Gor blimey, guvnor, if that's all you can afford I'll *give* you a bleedin' tie.'

And he would often present the bewildered man with a nice bright necktie, gratis.

Tosher never used 'plants' in the audience, he relied on his own inimitable style. Within minutes other people would be handing over money and Tosher would be selling ties like, well, like hot pies.

If he spotted a regular in the crowd – and in the 1950s I was often trudging the streets selling grocery products –

118

he would adopt an even more daring ploy. This involved producing a vast pair of tailor's scissors and seizing the regular's tie and cutting off the end!

'Now you got to buy, haven't you, you mean sod,' he would yell.

Such was his mesmeric hold over people I have never witnessed one person complain, not even mildly. He did it to me once – and promptly gave me three brand new ties.

It was extraordinary watching the crowd surge forward with their pound notes in hand, clamouring to buy. If you had asked Tosher what he knew about selling and marketing he would have snorted in derision.

'Load of old bollocks, mate, I'm just a street trader, never mind all this marketing crap.'

But he was a master of his trade, a brilliant, individualistic hustler who knew more about human psychology than a truckload of professors with degrees in Human Engineering.

When I was first Sales Manager of Westward Television in the middle sixties I used to make new salespeople come with me to see Tosher in action at Berwick Street market. We'd stand in the bitter cold and watch him unload merchandise to a muffled crowd at a prodigious rate of knots.

Sadly I haven't seen him for years, I don't even know if he's still alive. His spirit lives on, though; go to any street market and watch the modern 'Toshers' strutting the stuff. It's worth ten lectures at the Harvard Business School, and you'd better believe it!

21
Talk to the decision-makers – or how you can end up with sand in your suitcase

However much we breathe, eat, sleep and dream success, the hard facts of a salesman's life are that failure and refusal and, even worse, uncertainty, are ever-present spectres at the feast.

I know a salesman who has chosen to sell a very erudite and expensive financial investment package in Europe on commission only. He has thoroughly researched his market and knows that about one in a hundred prospects are likely to say 'Yes'. But to reach this golden nugget, this magical one per cent, he has got to pitch the other ninety-nine. What he sells requires patient and highly technical exposition. He has to argue with and persuade people of considerable standing in the financial community – many of them already wealthy and secure. But, as my friend explained, that *one* order is like a small win on the pools. He has taught himself to be resolute and unswerving in his rarefied world, and for the past seven years his earnings from *no more than fifteen* completed contracts have topped a million and a half dollars.

This is pretty unusual but it illustrates the most vital weapon in a salesperson's armoury.

Persistence.

You *must* be willing to press on and take the setbacks or you will *never* become a superstar.

You must also profit by your mistakes. Not by a maudlin

and self-destructive backward look at your most awful moments, but by analysing *where* you went wrong and *why*.

Don't look forward, however, to a golden era when you are so wise and persuasive that you will never make another foul-up: The important thing is not to make the *same* mistake twice. All salespeople can produce examples of the really monumental blunder, the devastating cock-up and the excruciatingly embarrasing moment. They make entertaining conversation around a candlelit dinner table, particularly when the other guests have a sympathy with the trade of selling.

The one that sticks in my mind, if not my throat, is a tale of wasted effort, high hopes dashed, international adventure and a touch of lunacy on the way. I repeat it here as an awful lesson to young sales-stars on the move who forget one of selling's golden rules: *unless you pitch to the real decision-maker your endeavours are as chaff in the wind*. I ought to have known better but I didn't. It happened like this. . . .

About eight years ago I was Sales Director for Westward Television, the ITV contractor for the South-West of England, and my boss was that charismatic buccaneer, Peter Cadbury. Cadbury had dreamed up a scheme which he believed would further enrich the company's fortunes and, as an incidental bonus, give us a bit of fun en route.

We were to provide Monaco-based Tele-Monte Carlo with an hour of English-language TV programmes each week, and in return I would sell hundreds of thousands of pounds' worth of airtime to international advertisers anxious to address themselves to the rich cosmopolitan audience strung out like a glittering necklace along the coast of the French Riviera.

No, you're wrong. That wasn't the monumental failure to which I was referring.

The Monte Carlo Caper, as Peter Cadbury and I

dubbed it, more or less paid for itself and we had some stupendous times flying into Nice in Peter's private aircraft and talking to Bulgarian princes, Jewish financiers from Edgware and canny Monegasques who spent more time in the casino than at their desks.

One day I was preparing to check out of the Hôtel de Paris in Monte Carlo after a two-day sales visit, when the concierge rang my room and informed me that there was a lady in reception who wanted to see me. Her name – I was informed in halting English – was Fiona Leigh-Smith.

Normally I will see *anybody* who is selling. My sympathy for kindred spirits, I suppose. But my plane was due to leave in two hours and I was anxious to get back to England. 'I'll see her on my way out,' I explained brusquely and continued packing.

Now the French Riviera in general and Monte Carlo in particular is notorious for pedlars of get-rich-quick schemes and I had met more than a few in my frequent visits to the principality. Nevertheless I rang for a porter, lit a Davidoff cigar and descended in the ornate lift to the stunning baroque foyer of the hotel.

There, sitting demurely in a skin-tight pink trouser suit, was a strikingly attractive redhead, clutching a wedge of files on her lap. Not unnaturally I strolled over and introduced myself.

Yes, she was Fiona Leigh-Smith and she did have a proposition for me.

Monte Carlo is a place where dreams come true, but on this occasion the lady had very serious intentions. She worked, it transpired, for a Middle-Eastern billionaire in Cannes who was well connected with the Saudi Arabian Royal Family.

Her husband, whom I met much later, was not only the skipper of the tycoon's yacht but also – and are you ready for this – the godson of a previous Pope!

After I had digested this mind-bending intelligence I suggested a light breakfast and a discreet bottle of champagne.

Over the scrambled eggs and '68 Krug Fiona unfolded her proposition. Would I like to set up a commercial television operation for the Saudis?

Her boss had expressed an interest in such a scheme and if it were properly presented he could sell it to the King. Now it is fair to record that at this stage the scheme was largely the brain-child of Fiona – an energetic and vivacious lady who found working on a three-million-dollar yacht for a fabulously wealthy foreigner fun but less than totally fulfilling. The lady was thinking laterally, trying hard to be original and creative and to inject her own life with a little bezazz!

There were, Fiona told me, some thirty thousand British expatriates resident in the desert kingdom and one of their most persistent enemies was boredom. Most of them were in Saudi on contracts which ranged from two to five years, and their prime motivation for being there in the first place was money. Large, tax-free incomes, plus free housing, servants and Mercedes motor cars were the sort of lures that drew engineers, chemists and quantity surveyors from the security of Surbiton and Leeds to the land of sand, oil and sunshine.

Fiona's boss, a very shrewd international businessman with considerable contacts, believed that an English-language television service – aimed at the Brits and possibly the Americans, and supported by high quality advertising – would achieve two vital objectives.

It would make the Saudi posting more attractive to those technicians and advisors upon whom the kingdom's economic future depended, and it would also enable native Saudis to learn the high-tech skills of running a television operation for themselves.

Clearly what was needed was a complete package – an entrepreneurial person or persons to put the whole thing together, costed, researched, resourced and viable.

As I sipped my champagne and ate my scrambled eggs, I entertained visions of wealth and prestige on a scale undreamt of even by Aladdin after he had snaffled the magic lamp.

It was but a moment's work to cancel my flight from Nice and re-book on a different airline later that day. I was gripped with an overwhelming sense of certainty. My company had the skills and the resources to set such an enterprise rolling. At a later date, I mused, we might need additional funding, but that, of course, would come from the Saudi Arabian treasury. Our involvement would be as contractors for the whole deal. We would provide the management skills, the marketing expertise, the programme know-how, the motivation. What at first appeared to be a very small operation covering at most one hundred thousand English-speaking foreign residents would surely grow until we were instrumental in setting up – for colossal management fees, of course – a whole Arabian TV network for the Saudis themselves. Our commissions from the sale of international advertising would run into millions of pounds alone. It is of such stuff that dreams are made. And frustrations.

Fiona and I strolled through the fabulous tropical gardens near the casino, talking earnestly about this great idea. Finally at noon we parted, she to return to her boss's yacht in Cannes, I to Nice Airport to catch a plane to London.

On arriving home I set about writing a preliminary plan of action. Research and costings, together with perhaps a feasibility study would come shortly afterwards. Speed was essential. Once it was known that a man in the King's confidence was being pitched for a major television scheme in Saudi Arabia, all manner of keen adventurers would throw in rival bids. The Americans with their vast resources could probably drown us, but if Fiona was right – and I believed she was – the key was getting the King's approval. This would come via her employer, who was trusted implicitly by the Royal Family.

At this stage of the narrative you may well be asking – why me? How come the delectable Fiona had chanced upon me when she could have contacted any of the world's major network companies like ABC, NBC, Thames or Granada?

Simple, really. During the hour of English-language television my company was providing each week on the Riviera I had appeared regularly in a series of promotional ads. My face was now well known and my company was clearly familiar with how to set up English programmes in a foreign environment.

On the following Monday I met with Peter Cadbury, and his reaction was typical and generous.

'It sounds as if it's worth a shot. You put the package together, research it and sell the concept to this mysterious financier and I'll see that we find the necessary start-up resources. If you blow it, you'll just have to abort and pick up the pieces.'

I lunched that day with a client of international standing at San Lorenzo in Knightsbridge. Over chicken Béarnaise and a bottle of chilled Frascati I sketched out my ideas about a full-service television operation in the Middle East. My client listened in fascination. Should such a venture come to fruition, he said, his company would certainly support it with advertising. They had a line of luxurious products in the games and leisure market that would suit expatriate Britons far away from home. He had in fact already advertised with us during our Monte Carlo

Caper and was just the sort of adventurous businessman we needed to attract.

Later that day I received another visitor in my office in Sloane Square, an advertising agent who had influence over several million pounds' worth of international business – and a man who had already created a market for design and printing in the Middle East for one of his specialist clients. He gave me further encouragement. I was now excited by the prospects and impatient to get the whole show on the road.

Working at high speed I spent the weekend at my desk in Surrey and wrote a complete position paper for the project. Before I could translate advertiser promises into hard cash I knew many hurdles would need to be overcome. First priority, however, was to sell myself to 'Mr Fixit', Fiona's boss, as the man most likely to succeed in such an extravagant enterprise.

A week later I flew again to Nice and took the short helicopter journey from the airport to Monte Carlo. The chopper skimmed along the coastline, past Cap Ferrat and a series of mouth-watering mansions belonging to the rich and powerful.

It was only after I checked into the Hôtel de Paris that I began to realise that actually meeting this critically important billionaire was going to be difficult.

This proved to be the understatement of the century.

His yacht, roughly the size of Harrods, was anchored in Monaco. He however, was in Rome, but was expected back within twenty-four hours. Thirty-six hours later he flew in from Italy in his private Lear jet, only to telephone from thirty thousand feet above the Alps to have his yacht meet him in Cannes.

I drove along the Côte d'Azur through traffic-choked Nice in order to clinch my appointment. By the time I had parked in Port Canto he was aboard but incommunicado.

Fiona was in Cannes, but not actually on the yacht. A huge man in a T-shirt, with muscles like Atlas, politely turned me away. Later Fiona phoned me after I had dejectedly driven back to Monte Carlo. Her boss, she explained, was an extremely busy man and it might make more sense if I went to Paris in a fortnight's time to see him at his office there. With hopes still relatively undimmed I returned to London and wrote a long introductory letter, explaining the outline of my proposal.

I had three copies made and posted: one to the yacht in Cannes, one to a poste restante in Paris and one to his 'occasional' house in London (a pitifully small twelve-bedroom job, valued at one and a half million pounds).

There was no reply.

With the recklessness born of misplaced optimism, I decided to fly to Paris unheralded and tackle the situation head-on. If I just showed up, I reasoned, my amazing powers of persuasion would surely transfix him and the deal would be on, if not exactly clinched.

One tiny problem presented itself. His forwarding address in Paris was a secret. Even Fiona, whom I telephoned, didn't know where it was.

'I've mentioned the idea to him,' she explained, 'but the only way to sell him anything is to see him face to face.'

I remember laughing like a hyena at this remark, having spent the best part of a month trying to chase a shadow.

A touch of detective work and two hundred francs to the bellboy at L'Hôtel in rue des Beaux Arts, revealed the following intelligence.

An Arab businessman of stupendous wealth had taken an entire floor at the Plaza-Athénée. Rolls-Royces by the dozen clogged the hotel forecourt and there were rumours of the man from Cartiers arriving with a trunk full of samples twice a day.

My man, obviously.

I caught a cab from the left bank to the Plaza Athénée and sauntered into the fabulous lobby.

There were more Arabs lounging about than the cast of Lawrence of Arabia. I selected one in a Savile Row suit and asked politely if Mr X was in the Hotel.

At this point I should confess that my pronunciation of complicated Arab names left a little to be desired and it is not unknown for several Middle-Eastern gentlemen to have similar-sounding names.

You know what's coming next, don't you?

On the fifth floor I was met by two more Arabs in full Rudolph Valentino costume. One of them appeared to have a diamond stuck up his left nostril. Either that or he was having trouble with his Vick inhaler.

I was shown into a sort of ante-room, devoid of furniture save for a velvet chaise longue. Another man with a vivid scar on his cheek gave me a glass of orange juice and a copy of *Time* Magazine. Half an hour later I was taken into another room, which looked like a converted bedroom, with a desk, chairs, telex machines, several telephones and a map of the world pinned to the silk wallpaper. Four men in immaculate English suits were drinking tea. None of them was my billionaire. I introduced myself. They smiled. What were my credentials? they asked with old-world politeness.

Credentials?

Could I prove I was British? Yes. I showed them my passport. Did I have the authority to act on behalf of my corporation? Of course I did. I was a director of a public company. I gave them one of my business cards. They read it as if it were the *Kama Sutra* and slid it back across the table. The card, they explained apologetically, was not sufficient evidence that I was a bona fide courier.

I thought, 'What the hell is going on here?' But said (with a grace to equal their own), 'Gentlemen, I have been trying to meet Mr X (I pronounced his name with exaggerated care) for several weeks now. A senior employee of his, based in the South of France has already appraised him of my intentions. All I ask is a chance to meet him man-to-man and discuss my proposals, which incidentally were sent to his yacht and his London house as well as his forwarding address here in Paris.'

One of the suits frowned and picked up my business card again. 'Mr Turner,' he said slowly, as if addressing an idiot of unpredictable temperament. 'Mr X has neither a yacht nor a residence in London.'

While I absorbed this neat little whiff of grapeshot, one of his colleagues produced a tin of lozenges and offered me one. I refused. Never take sweets from a stranger.

'Furthermore,' said the first man, adjusting what looked suspiciously like an MCC tie, 'we cannot fathom the connection between your television company and our request for written tenders associated with an animal health project in our country for cattle serum and sheep inoculations.'

'Funny you should say that,' said I, closing my briefcase with an authoritative snap. 'I do believe we've been talking at cross purposes.'

We shook hands solemnly and I left. To this very day I am convinced they believed I was an eccentric sensation seeker with mad designs to steal sand from the Sahara, using the television story as a cover!

Shortly after this Kafkaesque charade Fiona left the employment of the real Mr X and went to America.

I dropped all plans ever to locate him and filed my position paper among the unread novels of Sir Walter Scott.

The moral of this cautionary tale is clear. If you can't talk directly with the man who has the power to say 'Yes', then you may well end up wasting your time and energy talking to men with diamonds up their noses in Paris hotel bedrooms!

22
Giving your product personality – some lessons from medieval Venice

That the act of selling is as ancient as language itself may seem a faintly ponderous claim, but ever since men stood on their hind legs clad in animal hides, they found commercial transactions inevitable.

The cave-dweller bartered dried fruit in return for a freshly slaughtered pig – or even a son or daughter as a fair trade for a pair of strong horses. In each deal struck, there existed degrees of salesmanship or persuasion. Sometimes the vendor's enthusiasm would lead to exaggeration, even deceit – a lame horse passed off as sound, a store of fruit artfully arranged to conceal the maggoty centre within. As human nature rarely changes, the ranks of modern-day salespeople are just as likely to contain cheats and mountebanks as ever before. What has always fascinated me, however, is the instinctive *natural* salesman. In a previous chapter I mentioned the ubiquitous street traders of London's Soho whose art and timing are untutored, whose 'feel' for when to close a sale is impeccable. They possess all the proper ingredients which make the truly great salesperson – determination, quick wits, volubility and an instinctive knowledge of the human psyche.

I've seen these rough-hewn but spectacularly effective qualities in markets, bazaars and souks all around the world, and they seem to cross national, religious and cultural boundaries.

The great merchant adventurers of twelfth-century Venice who voyaged to exotic lands to buy silk and perfumes and precious metals must have presented their merchandise with enormous theatrical skill. Without in any way wishing to trivialise his historic achievements, Marco Polo, who was after all primarily a businessman, must have possessed a beguiling line in sales talk.

Curiously, the role of the merchant in old Venice was almost as respectable as the priesthood – many of the great art treasures, fabulous palazzos, monumental paintings and sculptures were either inspired by religious fervour or the private patronage of wealthy traders. Indeed, it is doubtful if Venice, the most stunning tribute to architecture and art in the world, would have reached its zenith without such patronage.

The history of Venice is crammed with colourful tales of how the great traders competed with each other and how they sought favours at the court of the Doge.

There are stories of silk merchants who, on returning to the city after years in the East, filled specially constructed gondolas with stunning displays of merchandise and hired troupes of musicians to follow in smaller craft and play rousing tunes while they stood in the prows of their own magnificent vessels, extolling the virtues of their goods. Now that, to me, is salesmanship of the highest order. Imagine the spectacle of those old merchants, beards plaited and waxed, exotic cloaks of fine silk billowing from their shoulders, their hands raised like prophets as they shouted above the wind and made their emotional sales pitch.

It is not difficult to believe the crowds living along the Grand Canal looked forward to these events as the next best thing to a carnival. The merchants would regale them with highly coloured tales of adventure in foreign lands, investing mere bales of silk with a kind of mystic aura.

The modern advertising practitioner would understand this as one of the fundamental rules of salesmanship – creating a 'personality' for your product. The more complicated and exotic the personality, the higher the price the product will attract.

Why is this so? In my view, it is because placing a 'real' value on something as intangible as product personality is nigh impossible.

In your local store today, at the perfume counter for example, you will find products which vary dramatically in price. Yet the fundamental difference between them is your perception of their 'personality'. There is nothing wrong in this, of course; it may be trivial, even self-indulgent to spend money on scent or after-shave lotion, but make no mistake, what you are purchasing actually transcends the physical properties of what is contained in the bottle. You are buying magic, quite literally.

Does that sound silly? Possibly, but if you think about it for a moment, when did *you* last buy perfume or after-shave because of its healing or therapeutic qualities?

In medieval Venice, one of the most highly prized products was zafran – often taking the form of a brick-shaped substance, orange-red in colour and moist and spongy to the touch. It had a myriad of uses, giving flavour to rice and colour to pasta. It was also the base for women's pomades and face creams, not to mention its popularity as an additive to perfume bath water. What was it? Well you will know it of course as saffron – it was made from the tiny stigmas of crocus flowers and it took hundreds of thousands of blooms to compress into the size of a brick. Labour-intensive and enormously expensive to gather, zafran nevertheless became, if you like, the 'Chanel No. 5' of ancient Italy. What appealed most about it, over and above its genuine and wide application as a flavouring and a perfume, was its pedigree and mystique.

So You Want To Be A Sales Manager?

Spoilt ladies of the Venetian court enjoyed being told that a mere pinch-bag of loose zafran had taken fifty labourers a whole week to gather. Today, the New York matron or Monte Carlo hostess likes to hear tales of rare new perfumes being drained from the scent glands of a mountain yak and transported in a refrigerated Lear jet to a bottling plant in Grasse.

If you think that's an exaggeration, just read a few perfume ads in the glossy magazines and you'll see what I mean.

Salesmanship is about investing otherwise mundane products or services with an aura which manifestly increases their desirability and thus their value. Just recently, I saw the marketing director of a 'natural water' company on a television programme. You wouldn't believe how enthusiastic this man was about one of nature's most simple elements. 'Our water,' he eulogised, 'is filtered through layers of volcanic rock from the very heart of a mountain. On its journey down, it picks up valuable minerals and mild salts that make it as fresh as an Alpine stream.' I remember thinking, This fellow is talking about *water*. Soon some smart Madison Avenue whizz kid is going to bottle air and promote as 'invisible but life-enhancing – captured for *you* from the mighty gusts that blow over the Dakota grasslands'.

Another ancient technique was to enhance a product's reputation by a cunning stratagem known as '*agravar*'. Although this phrase was much used in medieval Venice, it is in fact a Spanish word – roughly translated *agravar* means to add weight or make heavier. Thus a product such as a consignment of silk would be described by the merchant as being exotic or rare and he would develop its 'personality' by describing how he came by it and waxing eloquent over its fineness, its rarity and the hours it took to spin.

Agravar, or added weight, didn't mean the merchant leant on the scales or in any way changed the physical properties of the product. What he did, artfully, was to organise a 'plant' in the crowd who would, apparently spontaneously, claim wondrous or even fantastic benefits from personal experience.

I can best illustrate this technique by describing a typical market day in medieval Venice.

Imagine a cobbled square teeming with people, many of them huddled under the cool shadow cast by a vast clock tower. On a raised platform of rude planking, a merchant stands with two servants who are unrolling bolts of raw silk in dazzling colours. The merchant, bearded and dressed in extravagant robes, is winding up the crowd with his sales pitch. He gesticulates with heavily ringed fingers and tells in awe-inspiring detail how he had bargained with some Chinese or Arab brigand for his shipload of silk, how it had been spun by dozens of old women in some exotic location watched over by cruel overseers with whips and cutlasses.

In the middle of his spiel, the merchant caresses a particularly lustrous bolt and says, with slow deliberation, 'It has the same texture as a woman's thigh.' At this precise moment, the merchant's 'plant' cries out from the body of the crowd, 'Yea – and all who wear it against their skin will find good fortune in affairs of the heart. I purchased a stock of this same silk from the merchant here and all who wear it claim its efficacy as an aphrodisiac!'

At this juncture, the merchant chides the interrupter and scoffs gently at his claim, but the 'plant' will not be silenced. He develops his theme with vigour and conviction, even suggesting that a silk shirt tailored for a hideously deformed crouchback resulted in him receiving the amorous attentions of many pretty ladies. Again the merchant scoffs and returns to his main theme – but the

135

seed has been sown. 'Extra weight' has been added to the product, and by an apparently disinterested outsider.

The gamble pays off, there are enough gullible waverers in the crowd to start the bidding and at the end of an hour the merchant has sold his entire merchandise at twice its true value. Any fool who later complains that his love life has failed to improve since purchasing the silk can be honestly told by the merchant that *he* promised no such benefit.

I doubt if the technique would work today, although cynics may claim it is being practised in a more subtle form all the time.

It is not, however, a practice that I would commend, and the aspiring salesperson should stick to investing his product with more tangible virtues!

23
Elk stew, Nazism and the Berlin Wall – a cautionary note for enthusiastic salespeople

Salesmanship, or the art of persuasion, can sometimes become a dark and malign force when practised by charlatans, mountebanks or madmen.

This simple but unarguable fact struck me with some force a few years back when I was a delegate at an international conference in Berlin. After two days of relentlessly uninspiring debate at the Bristol Kempinski, a small group of us decided to hire a limousine and driver in order to explore the divided but fascinating city.

In our party was Peter Marsh, Chairman of Allen, Brady and Marsh, one of Britain's largest and most dynamic advertising agencies – and himself a supreme salesman of the most positive kind.

After an hour or so inspecting not very interesting monuments, we instructed the driver to take us into the strip of forest that hugs the perimeter of West Berlin. Here we chanced upon an extraordinary old hunting lodge which had been converted into a rather overblown restaurant specialising in game and raw German beer, served in quart-sized mugs.

The restaurant interior was like the stage set for *The Prisoner of Zenda*, with stuffed boars' heads mounted on the walls, dark, oily panelling and stags' antlers serving as hat-racks. A huge log fire crackled in the Teutonic-sized hearth and the waitresses wore dirndls and wooden clogs.

I am here to tell you that a meal of undercooked elk

stew, red cabbage and spicy black sausage the size of a marrow is not my idea of gastronomic heaven. Peter chewed his way through a piece of rubbery meat which was laughingly billed as wild boar steak and we all struggled with our foaming tankards of dark, bitter ale.

The proprietor, an immense fellow with a face hewn from teak and a belly that would have served as a bass drum for the Berlin Philharmonic, was visibly disappointed that we had failed to wipe our platters clean. Anxious not to upset him more than we had already, we fell to talking about 'the old Germany'.

'Hitler used to eat here,' he said suddenly, wiping his huge hands on a suspiciously bloodstained leather apron. We greeted this intelligence with less than rapturous enthusiasm and the landlord quickly added, 'But of course I only bought this place after the war.'

One of us, I remember, asked him if he had ever met the Führer, and he nodded cautiously. 'When I was a little boy,' he said.

The landlord cleared his throat importantly. 'Small, like this,' he said, extending his arm to shoulder height. 'But a good salesman.'

This curious remark has always stuck in my mind, and although at the time we all laughed, there is an awful truth in it that chills the blood. This dreadful little Austrian house-painter sold himself to the German people with a display of cunning, bombast and rhetoric that has seen no equal before or since. He must have possessed a sort of odious charisma that transmitted itself to the masses at those stunning rallies you see on old black and white newsreels.

We finished lunch with a little cognac, which at least dulled the fiendish flavour of the elk, and piled into our limousine, cigars glowing. At Peter's suggestion we then drove to the old Olympic stadium in the city – a vast and imposing symphony of concrete and steel that was the site not only for the 1936 Olympics, but also for some of the most spectacular rallies staged by the burgeoning Nazi party.

It was deserted when we arrived and an icy rain swept over the empty amphitheatre. It was not difficult to imagine it packed with eighty thousand cheering Nazis as Hitler and his henchmen stood on the podium beneath a gigantic red and black swastika, raising their arms in the now infamous salute.

Even those mute concrete pillars seemed imbued with a faint echo of palpable hysteria. We stood on that podium where the Führer had once addressed the faithful and it was an eerie experience.

'Imagine,' I said to Peter, 'the course of history might have taken a different shape if television had been a mass medium in Germany in the 1930s.'

With his dreadful skills as a hypnotic rabble-rouser, Hitler could well have seduced half the world if he had been spawned in the 1970s. We returned to the Bristol Kempinski Hotel in sombre thoughtful mood.

Hitler a salesman? Undoubtedly. He was the dark side of that same coin of persuasion that most successful businessmen seek to mint in their pursuit of profit and ever-increasing sales. He used, perhaps unconsciously, a number of techniques, theatrical and commercial, that are common currency among many whizz-kids in the business world today.

It is, of course, a matter of some debate whether whipping tens of thousands into a frenzy at a stage-managed rally is really salesmanship at all.

Billy Graham, the evangelist, is adept at crowd manipulation – although for vastly different reasons – and some of the other tub-thumping American preachers who now proliferate across that vast country are outstanding crowd psychologists. It is salesmanship, nevertheless. Not the kind of salesmanship that I would aspire to – or you, I hope – but we should recognise that it is a close relative of our trade.

Preachers 'sell' religion, and Hitler 'sold' Nazism – both activities driven and fuelled by fanaticism and a skilful way with words, gestures and selective argument.

It has been said many times before, but relentless determination *is* the backbone of all forms of selling; certainly Hitler and the Bible-punching Southern Americans in their five-hundred-dollar silk suits and fancy pink Cadillacs were brimming full with determination.

Non-salespeople will often describe determination as bloody-minded obstinacy, but I believe that is a glib oversimplification. In the world's most effective salespeople you will always find a diamond-hard core of determination. You may succeed without formal education, you may reach the top of the heap without finesse, social charisma, good looks, even without wit. But if you lack determination you are doomed from the start. Determination, as a single quality, reigns supreme. It is the raw fuel of success in many walks of life – not just selling.

I was reminded of this fact when later during our Berlin visit we were taken to see the notorious Berlin Wall – erected by a tyrannical regime determined to keep their citizens *in* rather than to repel marauders, and frequently breached by courageous people equally determined on their part to get out.

On the flight back to Heathrow I found myself reflecting on all I had seen during this short visit. The ghost of the insane salesman Hitler, still lingering between the concrete pillars of the old Olympic Stadium. The importance of determination as a critical factor in achieving almost anything in life – and the need to develop *only* these assertive, thrusting strands of the human personality in the pursuit of worthy objectives. Even the Oxford Dictionary's definition of 'determination' takes no moral stance – it simply states

Determination Firmness of purpose, the process of deciding or calculating

Be sure your own determination is directed to goals of which you can be proud. If you don't you could end up on the wrong side of a wall – or even spooning down a bowl of elk stew!

24
Is the customer always right?

There is a 'down' side to sales management, just as there is in every other walk of life. However exuberant your personality, however strong your resilience, however encyclopedic your knowledge and however persuasive your vocabulary, you will still have to deal with problems that land on your desk with the delicacy of a putrescent three-week-dead warthog.

One of your great tests, therefore – certainly in the eyes of your staff and your superiors – will be how you handle these all too frequent situations. They come in many guises, such as itinerant wives or husbands convinced that their particular darling is being given the bum's rush by a callously indifferent management – 'My Sidney has had stomach cramps and not a wink of sleep since you over-looked him for the Northern Area Manager's job' – and sometimes the little lady or gentleman actually shows up at the office, face streaked with tears, to plead their case in person. You think I jest?

Never underestimate the venomous proclivities of a spouse. In these circumstances you will need strong nerves and the icy control of emotions usually associated with free-fall parachutists or priests taking confession from a troupe of nymphomaniac axe-murderers. You will have to explain as gently as you can that however much you value Sidney or Edwina's qualities as a member of the team, it is clearly impossible for everybody to earn promotion at the same time. You will also make appropriate noises of sympathy and appreciation at their concern and indicate with a world-weary shrug that your job is to make the decisions and this has to be, occasionally, a painful and lonely business. Then you will have to get them out of the office as soon as decency will allow. Perhaps a cup of tea and a ginger biscuit. Never a gin and tonic – however much they sniffle and weep. Your objectives are to hear them state their case and to make it clear that nothing they say or do can ever influence your ice-cool business judgement.

Now, if you think all the foregoing is bubble and squeak, and that sales managers never get cornered by the relatives of staff, you are – my friend – in for a very rude awakening.

The good news, however, is that problems of this *specific* nature are rare, but they *do* occur, and the forward-looking manager should brace himself for their unwelcome eventuality.

A far more common problem is the complaining client. It matters not a jot, or even a tittle, whether the client is in the wrong or has a host of angels on his side – the *style* of your reaction must be precisely the same. Why is this so?

Well, let's turn the tables for a moment. *All* of us are clients from time to time, aren't we? We're clients of the gas board and the local restaurant and the travel agent and the garage that services our car, and we do *love* slagging them off, don't we? Come on, be honest. At your last dinner party or get-together at the pub, didn't *one* of your acquaintances amuse you with a tale of tradesmen's incompetence, airline clerks' buffoonery, or head waiters' impertinence? And didn't you trump his story with a tale of your own about cockroaches as big as turtles in your last Greek hotel or gas fitters who sat motionless for three hours in the kitchen swallowing gallons of tea while they waited for a springle joint to be delivered by another useless layabout from their service department?

The British, by and large, do *enjoy* complaining and, contrary to popular belief, they complain often. When you sit behind that elegant sales manager's desk with your two telephones and that oh-so-discreet Pirelli calendar, you will be on the receiving end of complaints you wouldn't have dreamt of in a millennium of Sundays. The big difference now, of course, is that *you* have to do something about them. In the past, when you adopted the role of client, the act of complaining was in itself a purging experience. You got it off your chest and felt very much the better for having done so. Remember, therefore, to let *your* client get it off *his* chest before you proffer your apologies or your excuses. And if you have done wrong, admit it. Gracefully. And make certain you actually do something about it as quickly as possible.

It's worth not forgetting that even clients are human. Sometimes!

25
Cunning Stratagems and the decay factor – or how to leapfrog to greater success

If the ultimate objective of all selling activity is to achieve a sale or secure an order, it sometimes requires a salesman to resort to cunning stratagems.

These, let it be said at once, are not the same as dirty tricks – although to the purist who regards all commercial activity as immoral they will be scarcely distinguishable one from the other.

All salespeople who are engaged in a business that relies on repeat purchases will have established some kind of rapport with their buyers. These buyers will assume a mild omnipotence in the general scheme of things and will, if not watched with glacial impartiality, become so vital to the salesperson's success that he will fail to observe their rate of decay.

What in hell's name is a rate of decay? I hear you snort.

In a state of comfortable over-familiarity with the same buyer, a salesperson may lose his or her cutting edge. Because of the relaxed camaraderie between the two of them, the salesperson may overlook the fact that an account is reaching its plateau, that the price obtained is 'softening' or that a cosy tendency to over-discount is creeping into the negotiations.

And, perhaps most dangerous of all, that the buyers's real authority to make decisions has been completely eroded. It happens all the time.

A good salesperson can sniff out this decay factor like a bloodhound.

Sometimes the buyer's clout has been usurped by a more senior executive in the company. More often than not the buyer has reached the limit of his or her purchasing discretion.

What follows is stagnation, a stunting of sales growth and an all too familiar touchiness on the part of the buyer if you suggest he or she is less in command than hitherto. We have all encountered the cry 'Don't go over my head!' which is part threat and part plea.

You must learn to sidestep this trap – for trap it undoubtedly is – and use your skill to reach beyond the decay factor to whoever now influences real purchasing decisions. This will not be easy. You may need to maintain the confidence of the old buyer for routine business, standard repeat orders, etc, but at the same time reach up to a higher plateau for your really ambitious projects which need big investment decisions.

It is in such situations that you will employ cunning strategems. Here is one example taken from real life. It may not suit every situation – indeed, it could prove dangerous in some – but the principle is worth remembering.

It happened to me recently, when an account of long standing began to exhibit decay factors. All our efforts to pump up our share of the business, which was worth in excess of £200,000 annually, were thwarted. The buyer's excuse was that his 'American parent company' held the ultimate purse strings and, although he was naturally 'straining every sinew' on our behalf, we had reached a vast plateau from which there was no further growth.

He also warned, ominously, that any attempt to 'go over his head' to the UK-based managing director would prove counter-productive. The delicate umbilical cord of our long-standing relationship would be stretched to breaking point.

I was familiar with the complex nature of this company, which we shall call Corporation X. And I knew that its paternalistic but hierarchical structure was in the shape of a huge pyramid.

At the apex was the founder and president, who, lo and behold, controlled 85 per cent of the shares. He was a Los Angeles-based, self-made multi-millionaire – and if he said two and two made seven, then highly paid executives in London, Paris and Tokyo all nodded sagely and replied, 'Of course, Mr President.'

He never saw salespeople. He was protected by a loyal household and he was 6,000 miles away.

I filed away this piece of intelligence and set about other equally pressing tasks.

Four months later, in early spring, I flew to the United States on a routine sales visit, spending four days in New York before catching the shuttle to the West Coast.

After checking in at the Beverly Hills Hotel I set about phoning my contacts in Los Angeles. There exists a sizeable British colony in Hollywood and they have prospered in the cut-throat jungle of media buying and selling against what at first glance suggests insuperable odds.

One of them, an old and trusted friend, joined me for a drink in the famous Polo Lounge and we spent an hour gazing at the parade of film stars, producers, directors, hookers and no-hope adventurers who make up its clientele.

Later we took off for dinner at Jimmy's – an elegant restaurant much patronised by wealthy businessmen in the music trade. The President of Corporation X, bored with the manufacture of his worthy but lifeless artifacts, had lately developed a keen – some would say fanatical – interest in the performing arts.

147

In short, he craved celebrity; he had money by the sackload, he had the power to make minions tremble on four continents and he had a vast estate in the hills above Los Angeles from which he directed the fortunes of his empire.

My friend, whom I had told about our problem, also had an oblique interest in the performing arts and told me that Mr X often threw parties for people in the music business, pop stars, violinists, composers and the seething nimbus of hangers on who surround them. The parties, I was informed, were superbly staged by the poolside and offered an abundance of Californian food and French champagne.

Yes, an invitation could be arranged, but with the one stern provision – I was not to come on too strong and mount a full frontal attack! That, my friend counselled, would not only screw up his own tenuous links with Mr X but probably result in my getting mauled by his jealous officers in England for such an act of feral treachery.

My invitation arrived three days later and I noted with interest that the party would commence at four in the afternoon. This kind of eccentricity is unremarkable in Hollywood and I sent my white slacks to the laundry for pressing in anticipation of the occasion.

As parties go it was pretty ordinary. I suppose I had expected a surfeit of glamour, pouting starlets, the Rolling Stones under a marquee, famous names from screen and stage, black butlers proffering white powder from silver sugar bowls and a certain amount of macho posturing.

What I found in the event was a cluster of record company executives and their wives complaining about the avaricious royalties certain pop stars now commanded as a quid-pro-quo for allowing their names to be published under a specific label. Most guests were soberly dressed by Californian standards: slacks, T-shirts and a plethora of white Gucci shoes.

I spotted one minor English pop star looking raggedly dejected in his little boy's dungarees and Mickey Mouse plimsolls, but all he wanted to talk about was football. Soccer is going through a kind of renaissance in Hollywood, fuelled no doubt by Elton John and Rod Stewart, and this particular young man – although much less known – was clearly following in their footsteps.

I had not travelled half way across the world to talk with a youth who looked and spoke like a retarded navvy, so I moved on.

The half-acre of lawns was rimmed by superb palm trees and far below, where the brown hillside opened in chasms, I could see the blue shimmer of the Pacific Ocean.

The President of Corporation X, a much younger man than I had expected, probably in his mid-thirties, sat in a cane chair by the poolside reading the *Financial Times*, apparently oblivious to the gentle hedonism that surrounded him.

A waiter dressed in a 1930s cinema attendant's uniform with gold tassels served orange juice and champagne, and I noted that the President drank only orange juice.

I was introduced and we chatted amiably.

Did I like Los Angeles?

Did I find it provincial after New York?

Had I read Graham Greene's latest novel?

Did I plan to see Nureyev, who was rumoured to be planning a performance of *Swan Lake* in the fall?

Weren't American motor cars gross? (He drove only European sports cars – Ferraris, Jaguars, Maseratis.)

I was both flattered and surprised at this erudite young millionaire's interest in the world outside Hollywood and his obvious grasp of life's more cerebral pleasures.

After casually mentioning that he was learning to speak

149

Chinese, he tackled me with sudden directness about my job and my mission in Los Angeles.

'Do you actually sell airtime for an English TV station here in California? I would have thought that most unlikely.'

Well, not exactly, I explained to him. My American trip was to see the way American ad agencies operated and to pay my respects to some of the huge American-owned corporations which spent big money with my company back in England.

'Who are they?' he asked.

'Procter and Gamble, General Foods, Colgate-Palmolive, Kellogg, Pepsi-Cola,' I said.

'Aren't they autonomous in England?' he asked shrewdly.

'Yes,' I said, 'but I've never been turned away by the American parent companies, they all really loved being called on by an English salesman and it never hurts to say "Thank you" in person.'

He grinned and lit a cigar. 'So are you going to thank me?'

'Thank you,' I said, and he laughed uproariously.

'How's business?' he then asked. 'I mean, with us?'

'It's OK,' I said, sensing an opening.

'Only "OK"?'

'Yes.'

'Why?'

I told him I thought the level of investment with our station was too small to develop the true sales potential of his product range.

'Is that horseshit?' he demanded.

'No. I believe the market in the South-West of England can be substantially expanded. But only if you spend behind existing sales – which are good, but static.'

He pondered this. 'Like Proctor and Gamble?' he said.

'Sort of,' I replied.

'What the hell do you want me to do about it?'

'Nothing,' I said, lying skilfully. 'I'm just answering your questions.'

'Now that is horseshit,' he said. 'Have a drink.'

This conversation then moved away on to the subject of popular music, and my views on Elton John, Wings and Led Zeppelin were solicited. I doubt if my responses added a whisker to his already encyclopedic knowledge of the music trade.

The party ran its predicted course and no further business was discussed. I was introduced to an extraordinary woman of sixty who was slim to the point of emaciation – except for her breasts, which were spectacular. She wore a halter-neck mini-dress which accentuated these twin features. Try as I might, I couldn't stop my eyes travelling to the banquet of cleavage she presented.

'Do you like them?' she said with all the casual indifference of a woman showing you a new pair of gloves.

I don't usually find myself at a loss for words, but on this occasion I was as dumb as a stone.

'Silicone injections,' she said in a conversational tone. 'I did it for my husband. He loves them.'

With that she turned and walked unsteadily away.

That sort of thing, I mused, could never happen in Budleigh Salterton.

Much later, back in rain-lashed London, I noticed a sudden marked increase in Corporation X's investment with our station. The regular buyer made much of this, claiming responsibility and credit for placing such a large order. We accepted this without demur.

But, intrigued, I phoned Los Angeles that evening and spoke to the President of Corporation X.

'Just ringing to say "Thank you",' I said. He was silent for a long time and then said, 'OK, Harry. You got what

151

you wanted. But listen, I got good people in London. They don't know that you and I talked in LA. Let them take the credit. Not you or me. Do you follow? And, Harry, take care of that investment, will ya?'

Then he rang off.

As far as I was concerned that was the end of the matter. I had reached the ultimate decision-maker, and it was obvious he had talked at length with his English colleagues to corroborate my version of the market situation and then issued one of his famous 'do it' directives.

What was nice about the man was the he would have been furious if I had used his discreet intervention as a ploy to humilate his people in London.

I never did and never would.

Sometimes invisible and secret influences are at work in all our business lives.

Be grateful for them. They can cut both ways, remember.

Bestselling Non-Fiction

☐ Everything Is Negotiable	Gavin Kennedy	£3.50
☐ The Cheiro Book of Fate and Fortune	Cheiro	£2.95
☐ The Handbook of Chinese Horoscopes	Theodora Lau	£3.50
☐ Hollywood Babylon	Kenneth Anger	£7.95
☐ Staying Off the Beaten Track	Elizabeth Gundrey	£5.95
☐ Elvis and Me	Priscilla Presley	£2.95
☐ Maria Callas	Arianna Stassinopoulos	£4.95
☐ The Ulysses Voyage	Tim Severin	£3.50
☐ Something Understood	Gerald Priestland	£3.99
☐ Fat is a Feminist Issue	Susie Orbach	£2.50
☐ Women Who Love Too Much	Robin Norwood	£2.95
☐ Rosemary Conley's Hip and Thigh Diet	Rosemary Conley	£2.50
☐ Intercourse	Andrea Dworkin	£2.99
☐ Communion	Whitley Strieber	£3.50

Prices and other details are liable to change

ARROW BOOKS, BOOKSERVICE BY POST, PO BOX 29, DOUGLAS, ISLE OF MAN, BRITISH ISLES

NAME. . . . .

ADDRESS . . . .

. . . .

. . . .

Please enclose a cheque or postal order made out to Arrow Books Ltd. for the amount due and allow the following for postage and packing.

U.K. CUSTOMERS: Please allow 22p per book to a maximum of £3.00.

B.F.P.O. & EIRE: Please allow 22p per book to a maximum of £3.00

OVERSEAS CUSTOMERS: Please allow 22p per book.

Whilst every effort is made to keep prices low it is sometimes necessary to increase cover prices at short notice. Arrow Books reserve the right to show new retail prices on covers which may differ from those previously advertised in the text or elsewhere.

Bestselling Fiction

☐ Saudi	Laurie Devine	£2.95
☐ Lisa Logan	Marie Joseph	£2.50
☐ The Stationmaster's Daughter	Pamela Oldfield	£2.95
☐ Duncton Wood	William Horwood	£3.50
☐ Aztec	Gary Jennings	£3.95
☐ The Pride	Judith Saxton	£2.99
☐ Fire in Heaven	Malcolm Bosse	£3.50
☐ Communion	Whitley Strieber	£3.50
☐ The Ladies of Missalonghi	Colleen McCullough	£2.50
☐ Skydancer	Geoffrey Archer	£2.50
☐ The Sisters	Pat Booth	£3.50
☐ No Enemy But Time	Evelyn Anthony	£2.95

Prices and other details are liable to change

ARROW BOOKS, BOOKSERVICE BY POST, PO BOX 29, DOUGLAS, ISLE OF MAN, BRITISH ISLES

NAME...

ADDRESS...

....

....

Please enclose a cheque or postal order made out to Arrow Books Ltd. for the amount due and allow the following for postage and packing.

U.K. CUSTOMERS: Please allow 22p per book to a maximum of £3.00.

B.F.P.O. & EIRE: Please allow 22p per book to a maximum of £3.00

OVERSEAS CUSTOMERS: Please allow 22p per book.

Whilst every effort is made to keep prices low it is sometimes necessary to increase cover prices at short notice. Arrow Books reserve the right to show new retail prices on covers which may differ from those previously advertised in the text or elsewhere.

Bestselling Fiction

☐ Hiroshmia Joe	Martin Booth	£2.95
☐ The Pianoplayers	Anthony Burgess	£2.50
☐ Queen's Play	Dorothy Dunnett	£3.95
☐ Colours Aloft	Alexander Kent	£2.95
☐ Contact	Carl Sagan	£3.50
☐ Talking to Strange Men	Ruth Rendell	£5.95
☐ Heartstones	Ruth Rendell	£2.50
☐ The Ladies of Missalonghi	Colleen McCullough	£2.50
☐ No Enemy But Time	Evelyn Anthony	£2.95
☐ The Heart of the Country	Fay Weldon	£2.50
☐ The Stationmaster's Daughter	Pamela Oldfield	£2.95
☐ Erin's Child	Sheelagh Kelly	£3.99
☐ The Lilac Bus	Maeve Binchy	£2.50

Prices and other details are liable to change

ARROW BOOKS, BOOKSERVICE BY POST, PO BOX 29, DOUGLAS, ISLE OF MAN, BRITISH ISLES

NAME...

ADDRESS..

....

....

Please enclose a cheque or postal order made out to Arrow Books Ltd. for the amount due and allow the following for postage and packing.

U.K. CUSTOMERS: Please allow 22p per book to a maximum of £3.00.

B.F.P.O. & EIRE: Please allow 22p per book to a maximum of £3.00

OVERSEAS CUSTOMERS: Please allow 22p per book.

Whilst every effort is made to keep prices low it is sometimes necessary to increase cover prices at short notice. Arrow Books reserve the right to show new retail prices on covers which may differ from those previously advertised in the text or elsewhere.

A Selection of Arrow Bestsellers

Prices and other details are liable to change

ARROW BOOKS, BOOKSERVICE BY POST, PO BOX 29, DOUGLAS, ISLE
OF MAN, BRITISH ISLES

NAME. . . . .

ADDRESS. . . . .

. . . .

. . . .

Please enclose a cheque or postal order made out to Arrow Books Ltd. for the amount
due and allow the following for postage and packing.

U.K. CUSTOMERS: Please allow 22p per book to a maximum of £3.00.

B.F.P.O. & EIRE: Please allow 22p per book to a maximum of £3.00

OVERSEAS CUSTOMERS: Please allow 22p per book.

Whilst every effort is made to keep prices low it is sometimes necessary to increase cover
prices at short notice. Arrow Books reserve the right to show new retail prices on covers
which may differ from those previously advertised in the text or elsewhere.

Arrow Health

☐ The Gradual Vegetarian	Lisa Tracy	£3.95
☐ The Alexander Principle	Wilfred Barlow	£2.95
☐ Health on Your Plate	Janet Pleshette	£4.95
☐ The Zinc Solution	Professor D. Bryce Smith	£3.50
☐ Rosemary Conley's Hip and Thigh Diet	Rosemary Conley	£2.50
☐ Understanding Cystitis	Angela Kilmartin	£3.50
☐ Goodbye to Arthritis	Patricia Byrivers	£2.95
☐ Natural Pain Control	Dr Vernon Coleman	£3.50
☐ The Natural Dentist	Brian Halvorsen	£2.95
☐ The Biogenic Diet	Leslie Kenton	£3.50
☐ Ageless Ageing: The Natural Way to Stay Young	Leslie Kenton	£3.95
☐ Raw Energy	Leslie & Susannah Kenton	£3.50
☐ No Change	Wendy Cooper	£2.95
☐ Fat is a Feminist Issue	Susie Orbach	£2.50
☐ Day Light Robbery	Dr Damien Downing	£3.99

Prices and other details are liable to change

ARROW BOOKS, BOOKSERVICE BY POST, PO BOX 29, DOUGLAS, ISLE OF MAN, BRITISH ISLES

NAME...

ADDRESS...

....

....

Please enclose a cheque or postal order made out to Arrow Books Ltd. for the amount due and allow the following for postage and packing.

U.K. CUSTOMERS: Please allow 22p per book to a maximum of £3.00.

B.F.P.O. & EIRE: Please allow 22p per book to a maximum of £3.00

OVERSEAS CUSTOMERS: Please allow 22p per book.

Whilst every effort is made to keep prices low it is sometimes necessary to increase cover prices at short notice. Arrow Books reserve the right to show new retail prices on covers which may differ from those previously advertised in the text or elsewhere.

Arena

☐ The History Man	Malcolm Bradbury	£2.95
☐ Rates of Exchange	Malcolm Bradbury	£3.50
☐ The Painted Cage	Meira Chand	£3.95
☐ Ten Years in an Open Necked Shirt	John Cooper Clarke	£3.95
☐ Boswell	Stanley Elkin	£4.50
☐ The Family of Max Desir	Robert Ferro	£2.95
☐ Kiss of the Spiderwoman	Manuel Puig	£2.95
☐ The Clock Winder	Anne Tyler	£2.95
☐ Roots	Alex Haley	£5.95
☐ Jeeves and the Feudal Spirit	P. G. Wodehouse	£2.50
☐ Cold Dog Soup	Stephen Dobyns	£3.50
☐ Season of Anomy	Wole Soyinka	£3.99
☐ The Milagro Beanfield War	John Nichols	£3.99
☐ Walter	David Cook	£2.50
☐ The Wayward Bus	John Steinbeck	£3.50

Prices and other details are liable to change

ARROW BOOKS, BOOKSERVICE BY POST, PO BOX 29, DOUGLAS, ISLE
OF MAN, BRITISH ISLES

NAME..

ADDRESS...

....

....

Please enclose a cheque or postal order made out to Arrow Books Ltd. for the amount
due and allow the following for postage and packing.

U.K. CUSTOMERS: Please allow 22p per book to a maximum of £3.00.

B.F.P.O. & EIRE: Please allow 22p per book to a maximum of £3.00

OVERSEAS CUSTOMERS: Please allow 22p per book.

Whilst every effort is made to keep prices low it is sometimes necessary to increase cover
prices at short notice. Arrow Books reserve the right to show new retail prices on covers
which may differ from those previously advertised in the text or elsewhere.